Penguin Crossword Puzzles

The Tenth Penguin Book of
The Times Crosswords

Also published:

The Tenth Penguin Book of
The Times Crosswords

Penguin Books

PENGUIN BOOKS

Published by the Penguin Group
Penguin Books Ltd, 27 Wrights Lane, London W8 5TZ, England
Penguin Books USA Inc., 375 Hudson Street, New York, New York 10014, USA
Penguin Books Australia Ltd, Ringwood, Victoria, Australia
Penguin Books Canada Ltd, 10 Alcorn Avenue, Toronto, Ontario, Canada M4V 3B
Penguin Books (NZ) Ltd, 182–190 Wairau Road, Auckland 10, New Zealand

Penguin Books Ltd, Registered Offices: Harmondsworth, Middlesex, England

First published in book form by Penguin Books 1989
10 9 8 7 6 5

Copyright © Times Newspapers Ltd, 1989
All rights reserved

Printed in England by Clays Ltd, St Ives plc
Filmset in Linotron Times

Foreword

The crosswords reproduced in this book appeared in *The Times* between September 1986 and June 1987. The puzzle is by a different hand each day of the week, so they vary considerably in difficulty, though not, one hopes, in consistency or fairness. The puzzles in this book are arranged similarly, and do not therefore become progressively harder. They include the work of twelve compilers in all.

It is surprisingly easy to forget the artful tricks compilers can get up to – indeed, some of us are floored occasionally even by our own clues in retrospect. As Robert Browning is said to have remarked of *Sordello*, 'When it was written, God and Robert Browning knew what it meant – now only God knows.'

For this reason, the occasional notes included in the solutions at the back, which are mainly to identify literary, musical, mythological and similar references, also explain the mechanisms of a few clues that have perplexed me when selecting the puzzles.

John Grant
Crossword Editor of *The Times*

The Puzzles

1

Across

1 Presented an account for wine in study verbally (8)
5 Note to change flag (6)
10 Clean though rough growth (5)
11 Plain individuals making insinuations (9)
12 'A dark illimitable ocean without bound, without—' (Milton) (9)
13 Operate on a joint? (5)
14 One turn produces only a tiny bit (7)
16 Such fruit is kept in water (6)
19 Tolerates backward rural areas (6)
21 Support beastly capital development in the Mediterranean (7)
23 Table for a sailor crossing the Line (5)
25 Ironical racialist issue (9)
27 Clever approach about parking and temporary shelter (9)
28 Coarse aggregate (5)
29 Report some soldiers delayed (6)
30 The fool mistreating roses he values (8)

Down

1 The occupant let the players in (8)
2 Good player's score on a horse superior to all others (9)
3 Endless dressing is provided for the bird (5)
4 Agitation of mind makes no-one book up (7)
6 Joining a non-drinker and suffering for it (9)
7 Course taken by a singer (5)
8 Surest to turn reddish brown (6)
9 He'll rely on others less corpulent (6)
15 To do with the electricity supply being intermittent (9)
17 Press vote for a medal (4, 5)
18 Learn, say, to confuse an examiner (8)
20 Relationship between matron and nurse (6)
21 Fibs about a youngster? That's an understatement! (7)
22 Dressing right can cause little depression (6)
24 At least a million people have this language (5)
26 Reprobate getting fare served up in the French way (5)

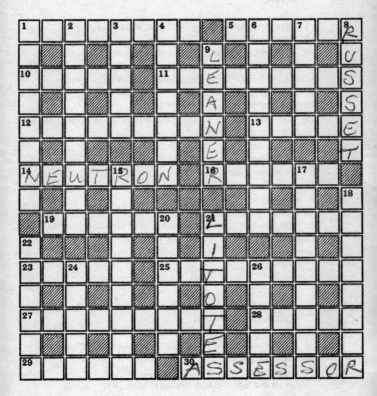

8 A... (faint clues, mostly illegible)
11 Con...
15 Foll...
16 Fre...
19 Th...
19 A b...
23 C...
27 C...

2

Across

1 After study, the battle's course is clear (8)
5 Get down fluid to the limit (6)
9 Take not a step out of line, before the numbers are known (4-4)
10 Spit in beer – the little devil started it (6)
12 Pours from more than one side, one is told (5)
13 Fail to finish trap for insect (9)
14 Convincing demonstration that ridiculous person needs fewer clothes (6, 6)
18 Sort of territory Cromwell gobbled up (12)
21 To run away twice – not like this soldier (6, 3)
23 Brown or black, there's uncertainty either way (5)
24 Account for former Israeli leader who called in the doctor (6)
25 Cat with a cough – a fearsome hacker (8)
26 The day the war ended, rabbit was about as import (6)
27 Back one who seeks to keep his title (8)

Down

1 Modest husband finds place in Indian social system (6)
2 Rabbit Jack could turn into a toad (6)
3 Description of human thumb is open to contradiction (9)
4 Accidental death coming between the motorways and the river (12)
6 No support for the leg in this dance! (5)
7 Draw out angle exceptionally small (8)
8 All enthusiastic at first, and in the fullest sense united (8)
11 Coup leads to seizure by boss (12)
15 Following out new order in anger (9)
16 Plague that affected half of France in poem (8)
17 The doctor's English, the poet admits (8)
19 A way to capture a snake on a ship (6)
20 City man not so well-off? (6)
22 Uplift revealed by bra is exciting (5)

3

Across

1 Stupefy with tot knocked back during social gathering (6)
4 Honour is given to worker showing respect (8)
10 Of course I can't rely on moving (9)
11 In German, one with a child is kind (5)
12 Often split, it could be claimed (7)
13 Capture retreating queen, and mate (7)
14 Make use of one in the union (5)
15 Belligerent Yanks (3, 2, 3)
18 Driver of train to provide a crew (8)
20 In flight, it goes straight up (5)
23 A zealot – in fact, a loony (7)
25 Philosopher concerned with a small group (7)
26 Forever it advises caution (5)
27 Tip from mum after she interrupts cook (9)
28 Points given to gnome for trying (8)
29 Put a note in for each petition (6)

Down

1 Face up to surrender (4, 4)
2 Wonder when drivers entered the race (7)
3 I'd get misled, taken in by compass misbehaving in fits and starts (9)
5 How to get sold a pup (or a cat)? (3, 1, 3, 2, 1, 4)
6 It ran divinely in classic horse-races (5)
7 Gas shells – the Scots own up (7)
8 'Erculean young blood shows up plain in the North (6)
9 Columnist can be upset by life among the lowly (5, 4, 5)
16 Meet criminal outside Alabama's capital on Thursday (9)
17 Board responsible for ditches (8)
19 Carrier gets U-boat in an instant to surface (7)
21 Cutting a dash outside, engineers put up with some rain (7)
22 A letter read out, and one to rub out (6)
24 Loopy boy (5)

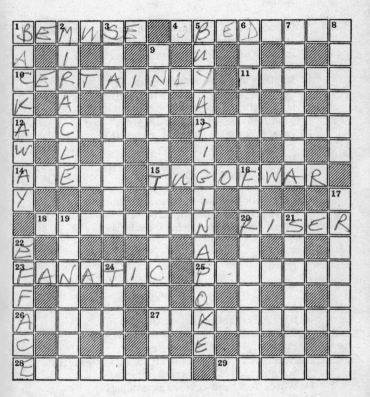

This puzzle was completed within 30 minutes by 25 per cent of the competitors at the 1986 London B regional final of the Times Collins Dictionaries Crossword Championship.

4

Across

1 Capacity of old vessel reduced by one quarter (6)
5 Hack writer produces worthless trifle (8)
9 Intimate what might be done, in fact (10)
10 Object sometimes dropped on pitch (4)
11 Singing style of latest composition (8)
12 One slew the albatross, as a result (6)
13 Having started with a will, you'll find it (4)
15 Transform rear of plane to fly (4, 4)
18 Party policy not one's main interest (8)
19 Punish schoolboy spectators (4)
21 Boatman taking over from pilot (6)
23 Display skill in flying machines (8)
25 Called for orange, peeled? (4)
26 Systematic though brief in examination (10)
27 Drive off from various tees round 25 (8)
28 My rhymes may be catching, on the surface (3, 3)

Down

2 Atmosphere of a native's capital (5)
3 Existing fashion (4-5)
4 It's barely required in some colonies (6)
5 Rex at home in children's game (4, 2, 3, 6)
6 Puts things in black and white, in PM's place (8)
7 Northerner's relations turned up just the same (5)
8 Scientist such as Democritus, for one (9)
14 Waves from snow-covered mountains (9)
16 Flower girl covered with stripes (5-4)
17 Judge in court producing outcry, so to speak (8)
20 Ringleader caught by an aged headmaster (6)
22 He may be said to have got the message (5)
24 Delicate basket (5)

5

Across

1 Nothing on it is calm – absolute farce, it turns out (8, 5)
9 Lichfield is such a city – see round it (9)
10 Swim length on stomach (5)
11 Honourable – and here in Rome (5)
12 Char in highland stream (4)
13 Disputes in banks (4)
15 Involving single action on those disturbed (3-4)
17 In Japan its skill is increasing, we hear (7)
18 Our mild version of a Kingston town band instrument (3, 4)
20 Newton – way-out name for a dark lady (7)
21 Endless gas in old recovery vessel (4)
22 Old money for a royal governess (4)
23 First signs of overs seeming inferior, expect runs from this willow (5)
26 One very large or very small bird – and tailless (5)
27 Seaboard churning up ocean silt (9)
28 Bat expected to hang in there at dusk? (5-8)

Down

1 Single-minded aesthete? (8, 2, 4)
2 Mahler's third in its entirety? (5)
3 Cor, blow me! (6, 4)
4 Underdone morsel in snack (7)
5 Port of New Orleans (7)
6 Principal bones of the foot (4)
7 Fancy garnish (9)
8 Theatre-designer of new features? (7, 7)
14 Distinguishing symptoms in dogs. I act with licence (10)
16 Instruct England's opening pair before and after the match (9)
19 Douglas's pet? (4, 3)
20 A river once more rises and falls (7)
24 Hip part of Troy? (5)
25 Here's a catch – tin covers silver (4)

6

Across

1 Cruel oppressor's son in regimental HQ (6)
4 Birkenhead boy, he – one leading many in battle (8)
10 Short piece? To a greater extent, I hear (7)
11 He may stumble on some sights worth seeing (7)
12 Moss for one received right coded message (10)
13 It sounded suitable once for a boundary (4)
15 Bar under fire at a North Dakota club? (7)
17 Deny acquisition of wealth, for example (7)
19 Quick notes for slow movement produced in seconds (7)
21 What, in Rome and Paris, Society uses for money (7)
23 Obscure old land area (4)
24 Description of Vasco da Gama's man-of-war? (10)
27 They make us sick in one vehicle when returning (7)
28 Splendid publicity for the old man! (7)
29 In a word, it's for bearing later – not unnaturally (8)
30 Suspicious about love divine from cheapjack (6)

Down

1 100 deserters under protest from Jefferson's party? (9)
2 Deviated from 18, maybe, the old having departed (7)
3 Higher than the monarch, say, yet cast from power (10)
5 Unnaturally sleepy, has untied right lace (9)
6 Succeed in getting hold of a metal spike (4)
7 A leading lady – the newspapers are after half of them (7)
8 Student leaves titbit for a walrus (5)
9 Diggers find this stopper useless (4)
14 A form of homage prim characters reproduce (10)
16 Old man in a dither – an Iraqi churchman, possibly (9)
18 One of Macbeth's precursors to dusty death (9)
20 Fundamental aid distributed in river state (7)
22 University awaited judgement being drastically affected (2-5)
23 Popular number about Jack's costume (5)
25 Dress needs a nether garment (4)
26 Aspersion on those who mostly eat noisily? (4)

7

Across

1 Take the air in a cab with me, perhaps (8)
5 Schoolboy who doesn't have rows (3, 3)
10 Katie Glover, blonde from Australia? (4, 4, 2, 5)
11 Narrow neck – a typically Corinthian feature (7)
12 From the P R angle, somehow it helps in a marine take-over (7)
13 Roman poet had silks in vermilion (8)
15 Smooth intersection (5)
18 Vehicle or horseback – either will do (5)
20 Single knot soundly spliced (8)
23 In French hearts they are cries for more (7)
25 Poor Clio, seized by bird from home of the Muses (7)
26 £1 avocado dinner cooked for polymath (8, 2, 5)
27 Joint in double-breasted jacket (6)
28 Move up to fetch in van (3, 5)

Down

1 Business liaison (6)
2 Standing up in herring boat's stern (9)
3 David gets no supplement as a recipient of charity (7)
4 Slices approach shots (5)
6 Note the machinery's going to pot again (7)
7 Beefy peer? (5)
8 He observes the hive, might one say? (8)
9 Bank on the Spanish using irregular measures (8)
14 Bottom team is beneath support (8)
16 Reserve the ice centre for a dance (9)
17 Former red mole left in disarray (8)
19 Dashed upset over charge for recount (7)
21 Black lady in Illyria? No, in S America (7)
22 Release from a foreign bore (6)
24 Chopped spice (5)
25 Johnson's pet rustic (5)

8

Across

1 Means buses can't move (9)
6 Agree to strike (5)
9 Swarms appearing since about spring (7)
10 The proposition Edward set out (7)
11 Poet occupying a loft? (5)
12 Not even one of the Baker Street boys (9)
13 Taking rest, lies sprawling, so is never weary (8)
15 Assistance for the man with a record (4)
19 Starting in chiropody, treat only a part of the foot (4)
20 'Present mirth hath present—' (*Twelfth Night*) (8)
23 Risk coming by river (9)
24 Concerned with a dog that's come at intervals (5)
26 Overhead lines (7)
27 A country music man (7)
28 Deposit for a house (5)
29 An orange or possibly a green tin (9)

Down

1 Peg that is loose in Italian strings (9)
2 Flower trade improvement – there's money in it (5)
3 They allow certain plants to get a firm hold (8)
4 Wine in the home? Most objectionable! (8)
5 Able to bring parking into use (6)
6 The cost of an attack (6)
7 Being in command etc perhaps calls for a mental faculty (9)
8 Duck in the Schleswig-Holstein river (5)
14 Felt better and got dressed again? (9)
16 Some crest! Some bird! (9)
17 A Roman Emperor's bloomer (8)
18 Changing gear, give trouble (8)
21 Writing the hotel a note is quite natural (6)
22 Start in error with the collection (6)
23 Benefit a few and suffer for it (5)
25 Jacket one made from raccoon-like animal (5)

9

Across

1 The aitch is articulated when it precedes a hero's home (6)
4 Collect what's been thrown away – in other words, get one's own back (8)
10 Two blues for hearties (5, 4)
11 In introductions, nobody ought to call Harry Nick (5)
12 Lace – half a guinea to clear (7)
13 Printer's sort of rule man breaks (7)
14 Letter that he takes to heart (5)
15 Musicians in costume (8)
18 Story a bird carries on (8)
20 What could grow around lake's southern shore (5)
23 Criticize long dash (7)
25 Will the merry man . . . (7)
26 . . . furnish pantomime's finale with a jest? (5)
27 Drafts posted to carrier are given anti-skid footwear (9)
28 A few lines are unreasonable (8)
29 Return with rapture to leading town in Devon (6)

Down

1 Cross about engineer getting water (8)
2 We got involved with hairy bats (7)
3 State appealing about another state's judge (9)
5 Most of you set your scene in order to show deep emotion (3, 4, 4, 3)
6 Malevolence responsible for capsizing ship I boarded (5)
7 An idiot is not sharp (7)
8 Draftsman's fallen into river – empty the lungs (6)
9 A part of geese I'd fancy (4, 2, 4, 4)
16 'Hair' – hot musical, no end original (9)
17 Try and invest money soundly in us – we'd protect investors (8)
19 Monkey, given nothing to eat, exhibits listlessness (7)
21 Walk slowly up to top of hill, home for Arion's rescuer (7)
22 Maintenance increased? Then hold back (6)
24 Gets the point, would you say? (5)

This puzzle was solved within 30 minutes by 14 of the 22 competitors in the 1986 national final of the Times Collins Dictionaries Crossword Championship.

10

Across

1 Flannel is more spread out (7)
5 Impressive capital of Alabama? No, of another state (7)
9 Rule about soldier's return to quarter (5)
10 A nut roast cooked for a high flier (9)
11 Welsh support for what's pledged in song (6)
12 Rustic makes a stir with GCE reform (8)
14 Losses from strikes (5)
15 Bitter end to speech (9)
18 Northern Ireland, wherein distillery produces drink (5, 4)
20 Anthem coped with without books (5)
22 Extraordinary eastern policeman (8)
24 Right to support monarch (6)
26 The criminal is also a healer (9)
27 A single girl going about in the Highlands (5)
28 Get job with Egyptian navy by the back door (7)
29 Changed broken treadle (7)

Down

1 Half the elements needed for strong liquor (4-5)
2 David's wife asking for a stiff drink (7)
3 State named in cross-head above middle of speech (9)
4 Didn't walk noisily in the highway (4)
5 The lager to change to, on the whole (10)
6 Little man from Zurich (5)
7 Austere Pole meets Brown (7)
8 High living for this wit (5)
13 Iberian girl soundly beat boy (10)
16 Artist, engineer and doctor affected by form of alcoholism (9)
17 Then, sadly, two little boys got raised aloft (9)
19 Mark should have a pronounced effect (7)
21 More intoxicating than some cakes? (7)
22 Bar from the latest OPEC meeting (5)
23 Warning about right to beg (5)
25 Point to a portico (4)

11

Across

1 Ulysses's concession (5)
4 Delayed, Giles staggers in to pass Bill (9)
9 Does he succeed by will-power? (9)
10 Poetically under a Welsh town (5)
11 Sombre at first and dark, but not in shadow (6)
12 Point in favour of antelope (8)
14 Jack takes the Spanish award in scientist's honour (5, 5)
16 Attempt to wound (4)
19 Sort out remains of meal (4)
20 A nature ill-disposed and one-sided (10)
22 What a faithful wife, to run off with a writer! (8)
23 A bit of a rash politician, to be found in a stately home (6)
26 Pawnee relative? (5)
27 Ballet posture of Lincoln in square dance (9)
28 Gruff, maybe, finding butter behind the teapot (5-4)
29 Short melody from the 'Messiah' (5)

Down

1 SOS! Lading is slipping and sliding about (9)
2 An envelope for Lady Grey (5)
3 After hill work, have a maize-cake (8)
4 Hearing impediment of Baltic statesman (4)
5 Ugly sister to French author has blue veins (10)
6 Lines my boy used for fishing (6)
7 Small research place in a plant for ornamental material (9)
8 Turn up information about hospital investment, say (5)
13 Hammers are used here to get impressive quiet (5, 5)
15 Maybe a well-stocked garden is strange to Caliban (9)
17 Apollo's summerhouse? (9)
18 Dispatched to gather up mud from grating (8)
21 Dwarf pear, perhaps (6)
22 It sounds a well-paid position (5)
24 Nettle patrol has no end (5)
25 The intelligence to circumvent a delay (4)

11

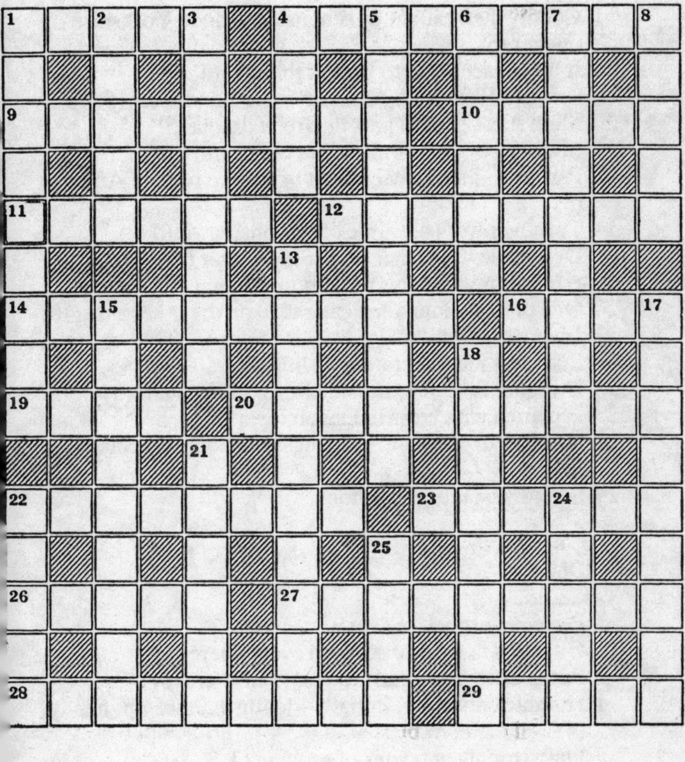

12

Across

1 County men caught by other side include Yorkshire opener (5)
4 It helps racehorse to be first to jump (4, 5)
9 So-called writer might alarm some Londoners (5, 4)
10 Main star's central part in Greek drama (5)
11 Majority of the people in the old country (6)
12 Part in Hamlet or Merchant of Venice back in America (8)
14 Turnover from a couple of seasons, say (10)
16 Does have as partner such a speculator (4)
19 At short notice, sent back information (4)
20 One of lucky foursome caught 50 on the other side (10)
22 Jibes without difficulty as island appears (8)
23 Like Mercutio's scratch, no huge disaster (6)
26 Our gunners left us outside range of Russians (5)
27 A church with cross in Devon town (9)
28 Member of temporary alliance given blanket coverage (9)
29 Soundly beat one in school (5)

Down

1 Perfectly proficient? (9)
2 Quality a mariner discerned everywhere (5)
3 Put in after firm's start to create easy job (8)
4 Humble employee, initially – loathsome scamp, finally (4)
5 Play strongly in favour of nothing (3, 3, 4)
6 Dog, a matchless sort of boxer (6)
7 Successful candidate contrived 90% in paper, I note (9)
8 Alexander's beloved Asians (5)
13 Liberal crossing the floor, as 27 might be (4-2-4)
15 Ticket collectors' nemesis (5, 4)
17 Unusual foresight, as exemplified by Pegasus (4-5)
18 Latest play and novel (5-3)
21 Her intelligence provided James with title (6)
22 Advertisement for a jacket (5)
24 Like difficult radicals at heart (5)
25 Northern (or Southern) sea-bird (4)

30

This puzzle was solved within 30 minutes by 15 of the 22 national finalists in the 1986 Times Collins Dictionaries crossword championship.

13

Across

1 Cabbage work-rate, perhaps, of the beetles (10)
6 Home fixture for City (4)
10 Short-backed college servant is down-at-heel (7)
11 Salesman in charge of the kettle department (7)
12 Get engaged to make synchronising mechanism (9)
13 It has to go back before the tenth (5)
14 Disappear from Barchester Towers? (5)
15 It is designed to stop beans over-baking (3-6)
17 Side above water release directors (9)
20 Moving arm in two directions (5)
21 Harmful substance found in canned beef (5)
23 Vendor apt to renovate such a sale-room piece? (9)
25 Holy character and sort of saint, this musician (7)
26 Ron gets duck – lbw – out to such a poor delivery (3-4)
27 Capital architect using northern wood (4)
28 Deposit New York paper met somehow (10)

Down

1 Grainless tropic island (5)
2 Merry and bright (9)
3 Machine for which barmaid need not give change (3-5, 6)
4 Strong bands, not elastic (7)
5 Brave, having symptom of erythema (7)
7 Confess one's escaped from Maidstone somehow (5)
8 Countryman presenting his ears? (9)
9 Bur to irritate (3, 3, 5, 3)
14 This fastener makes us secure, workin' in office (6-3)
16 This is meant to show the correct time in bars (9)
18 He approves of true accounts (7)
19 Elaborate work in the dark (7)
22 Hospital's cross-beams? (1-4)
24 Opinion of English into Spanish wine (5)

14

1 Drilling site (6, 6)
9 Sort of transport liable to ill usage (9)
10 By no means all pay minimal tax in this country (5)
11 Maintain a member in drink (6)
12 Apprentices the boss sent on new course (8)
13 Having caught it in the river, cause quite a stir (6)
15 Get well-qualified group (8)
18 King has priest cast off and smacked (8)
19 Pretend to have some influence (6)
21 Usually firm only after midsummer (8)
23 A shooting box (6)
26 Trainee (male) has it in him to be flexible (5)
27 Food diverted into Turin (9)
28 But woman's hilarity is not occasioned by crime (12)

Down

1 Win over a hundred in a horse-race (7)
2 Show resentment concerning level of noise (5)
3 Representatives get sealed orders (9)
4 The company go for the Scotch! (4)
5 A musical proposal? (8)
6 Being turned over, Edward is baptized (5)
7 Stretch a leg and note outcome (8)
8 A little girl's story about a donkey (6)
14 A strike in town would be a disaster (8)
16 Fed-up with being a consumer – it's frustrating (9)
17 Charges about a swimmer's sympathies (8)
18 Remember to telephone again (6)
20 The coach for rough terrain (7)
22 Noted play (5)
24 'All we have willed or hoped or dreamed of good
   shall—' (Browning) (5)
25 Egghead sending up worker may cause an eruption (4)

15

Across

1 Characters preceding MP sob for her (5)
4 City laid out under big hill, initially (9)
9 Test match? Final defeat (9)
10 English composer's wrong in bar (5)
11 Not a full house before main book writer appears (5)
12 Mundane description of traveller in space (9)
13 The rest making upstart live outside (7)
15 Attractive artwork (7)
18 Some day for it, perhaps? So they say (7)
20 Satirist finds half the jury bribable (7)
21 Plain black? *Au contraire!* (4, 5)
23 Scrounge old coin found in lift compartment (5)
25 Boxer's feet, say, stop moving briefly (5)
26 Veteran bats, e.g. at Lord's (3, 6)
27 Cosmetic device? Yes, had owned some (3-6)
28 Took out old hat (5)

Down

1 Start fighting to secure some brass (4, 5)
2 Fish below end of pier – using these? (5)
3 Dangerously silly way walk takes in road (9)
4 Liberal supports what's in text, for instance (7)
5 Country in which I touch down again? (7)
6 Borrow travel book, this one in Spain (5)
7 Are you and I said to lead race? What a disaster (9)
8 Convenient for Hungary's borders (5)
14 Authentic 18th century character (5, 4)
16 Publicly supported case, in short, in a 28 (9)
17 From route to Samarkand remove a plant (9)
19 Area inside American bases (7)
20 Flying squad needed to catch this thief? (7)
21 Wood he put round piano (5)
22 Seaside area, say, involved in mast production (5)
24 Appreciate it may be short measure (5)

15

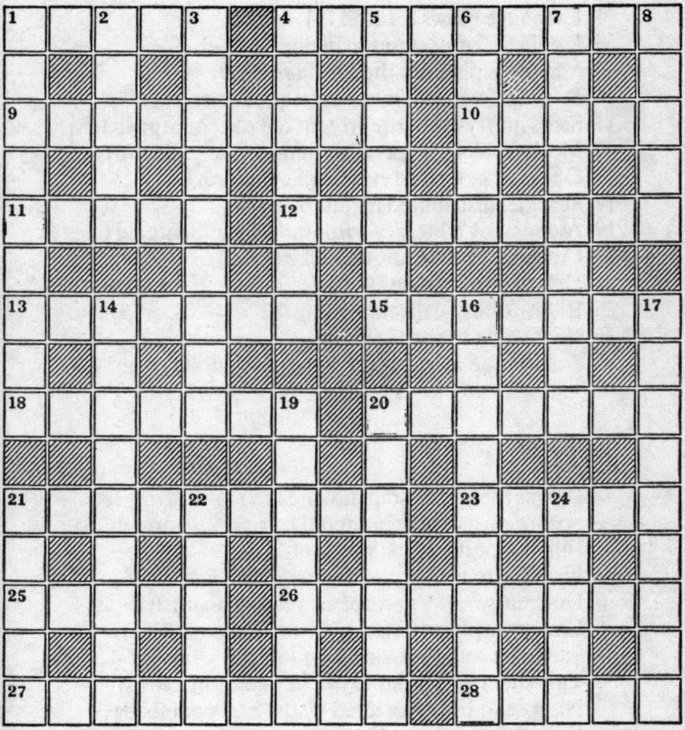

16

Across

1 Exchange blows for a bit (5)
4 Pythia for one set out to divide the mob (9)
9 Michael's place on the Dvina river (9)
10 Derived from a number at frequent intervals (5)
11 Scots marry and/or represent the old county (4, 3, 8)
12 Muslim chief accepts extermination schedule (6)
14 Obstruct new cart reversing in the farm (8)
17 Set spiel distributed in letters (8)
19 A denial by a literary corporal – an unidentified one (6)
22 City once named after a rock? (5, 10)
24 Help to make a curtain, say (5)
25 Ruling odds I call stimulating (9)
26 Neat guide to craft? (9)
27 Sounds like a little girl, this supernatural servant (5)

Down

1 Cabinet supports step designed to make flights secure (9)
2 Strong currents encountered by river champions (5)
3 Bill, the port authority eccentric (7)
4 In which to worship a deity in Pennsylvania? (6)
5 Unhealthy rainy parts of an ancient region (8)
6 Circus proprietor who's new to an island (7)
7 Set down soldiers in harbour (9)
8 Two characters from 22 *dn*, or one from 11? (5)
13 Dispose of bird protected by the best people (9)
15 Eg US politician eager to upset Establishment leaders? (9)
16 See about novice – one in mineworkers' element (8)
18 Gossip makes up story about Rechabite king (7)
20 Someone's tin god making a retreat! (7)
21 Individual appearing in it is all there! (6)
22 Guy's remains? (5)
23 Agreement about leaving a French island (5)

17

Across

1 By name, the river of Liverpool (6)
5 French socialist is haughty, being a viscount's son (8)
9 One who applies squeeze to corrupt the jury? (8)
10 E African policeman to demand terrorists' return (6)
11 Leading goody-goodies in by midnight (8)
12 Dicky back in lodgings looking wan (6)
13 Returned one spilt tea as waste (8)
15 Backward S African village needs stimulus (4)
17 One of five runners in alertness test (4)
19 Intra-mural chamber – suit married partner (8)
20 Football side goes hard in violent attacks (6)
21 Near mink, produced in the Crimea (8)
22 Disreputable drunk loose, we hear (6)
23 Joint projections over which one may get rapped (8)
24 Sudden charge forced down in Kent perhaps (8)
25 Fraudulent Teuton held (6)

Down

2 He can assemble Royal Marine police (8)
3 Ahead in the game, American applauded from dug out (8)
4 Mexican dish originating from Chaldean one (9)
5 Old foreign preserve for Gamaliel's titled son (9, 6)
6 Put at a disadvantage opposite down platform (7)
7 Large type of banner, for example (8)
8 Get a definite promise to fix floor (4, 4)
14 It's worn by the athlete – the lines appeal (5, 4)
15 Honourable words left in for Shakespearian braggart (8)
16 Baroque cupolas round university are little works of art (8)
17 Pooh's relations getting very high hat (8)
18 Manifest in up-bringing of father – mother too, maybe (8)
19 Snatch the sauce (7)

18

1 Unprofitable attachment in old mother's household (8, 4)
9 Second chance to see the sport when gunman is attacked on board (4-5)
10 Peer was one of three in the pound (5)
11 Officer holds up a dome (6)
12 Gammadion, was it? Ask for reconstruction (8)
13 Tether the latter part back round a ram's head (6)
15 Kind of band seen by a road – 'army' band? (8)
18 Girl's dried fruit everyone rejected (8)
19 Wind snakes round about (6)
21 Having finished, send out return of extra work done (8)
23 Worker let out Kipling at school (6)
26 Yet it used to show the name of Paul's companion (5)
27 Many guineas won at this card-game (9)
28 Enter an actor – one seen in a music centre (6-6)

Down

1 Left for South in S American capital to find wild cat (7)
2 Make smart coppers surround the border (5)
3 Alice's lot going crazy with swing (9)
4 It's used to catch river fish (4)
5 Evangelist has support of cordial Laodicean (8)
6 Dickensian taxidermist as space-traveller (5)
7 Faced being beheaded. A bit tricky. Give up? (8)
8 Local tax raised without being paid. It could create an explosion (6)
14 Gambling allowed in the course of one's journey (8)
16 Mississippi's capital (so-called) not used in prison construction? (9)
17 Roman priest takes care of the dance (8)
18 Quickly getting right on top in a riot (6)
20 Sportswear for the honest village blacksmith for instance (7)
22 A little honey that jeopardized Jonathan's life (5)
24 Wine given to girl (5)
25 Due to hear something from Horace (4)

This puzzle was solved in a record 4½ minutes at the 1986 national final of the Times Collins Dictionaries Crossword Championship by Mr David Armitage, aged 21.

19

Across

1 In short this is the day to make one (9)
6 Model acted for younger brother (5)
9 Forty minute job for Robin to describe it? (7)
10 Publication appearing stage by stage (7)
11 Supplementary rate vote is out of order (5)
12 Submission for an award to daughter and niece, perhaps (9)
13 Sombre but done with style (8)
15 A kiss can be a carrier, they say (4)
19 Original plot? (4)
20 Does one need leave to do this? Yes (8)
23 The importance of star rating (9)
24 Discover poet and knight (5)
26 To do with water in the wine (7)
27 Sweet noise made by actors? (7)
28 One of an opening pair (5)
29 Support for the working artist (9)

Down

1 Long-faced dismissal of Cassandra's tidings? (9)
2 'I—it, said the Carpenter,' (Carroll) (5)
3 Opening for transport? (8)
4 Creature with resting place on river (8)
5 Republic takes in nothing but farmers (6)
6 Police are about and impartial (6)
7 Bond girl's neuter disguise (9)
8 Experience a smack (5)
14 Always go for this type of growth (9)
16 Swift runner in the first fifteen? (9)
17 New look for examination? (8)
18 A minister's assistant receives praise. Cheers! (8)
21 Do this in arithmetic to rule (6)
22 Cattle county (6)
23 Walk briskly in Cambridgeshire (5)
25 A household name in the orchestral world (5)

20

Across

1 Puny son, often washed out (6)
4 In confusion, lops head of everlasting flower (8)
10 Urchin learning to beg (7)
11 Fish farming in bays (7)
12 Rollers bringing fish to the table (10)
13 Sir Andrew's sort of impudence gives one a fit (4)
15 Sound pitch, but on one spot it's getting thinner (7)
17 Field force unit concealed in E Dorset (7)
19 He interprets outdated notes about contract (7)
21 Feared movement to the left of central government (7)
23 Guide pointing to the light (4)
24 Cricket side delicately tapping the ball – how disconcerting! (3-7)
27 Stop, change to amber, then green (7)
28 University man accepts married Italian (7)
29 Put too much value on speed of deliveries (8)
30 Blackbird used to chase hares (6)

Down

1 Neat jelly at the bottom of the packet, perhaps (9)
2 Pacify vegetarian animal (7)
3 Protection for the Chair from mud-slingers? (5, 5)
5 Is sweetbread a prominent feature in Brazil? (5-4)
6 Listen hard to chest (4)
7 Some men taken for a drink (7)
8 Left sharp side of rock projecting (5)
9 Surgeon with nothing to say no to (4)
14 Praiseworthy arrangement to clear one debt (10)
16 Soldier wouldn't look right obeying this order (4, 5)
18 Application for a stage-coach (9)
20 Not changing uniform (7)
22 Abusive language from a fence (7)
23 Professed faith in sacred offerings (5)
25 Fish look sullen (4)
26 Brother to Uncle Remus (4)

21

Across

1 Lose money converting carbolic to this kind of acid (7)
5 Transport mediation service? Capital! (7)
9 Workers, never back to the fore, who return to haunt us (9)
10 Means of communication with a walrus (5)
11 Australasian in turn declaring himself a wanderer? (5)
12 Laced it in differently, but just the same (9)
14 Perhaps one said as a metaphor (but could just as soon be written) (6, 2, 6)
17 In TV we hear gentlemen taking first class return are the brainy ones (14)
21 Half-moon (9)
23 Jack the menace becomes half-hearted nearer maturity (5)
24 Lamb-like in appearance, Ophelia namely (5)
25 Residence provided by London Stock Exchange? (4, 5)
26 Is Africa doubly so just before dawn? (7)
27 Give new form to both sides, including oriental style (7)

Down

1 A couple of rows for its oarsmen (6)
2 Course for music-maker in composition of air (7)
3 Argument against the French one raised – always happening (9)
4 In view of Wagner's work being led by study team (11)
5 Trigonometrical ratio of an Aegean island (3)
6 Send the man with the stop-watch up (5)
7 Many an obscure utterance in this ancient craft (7)
8 Furtive sort of hat style (8)
13 Tour de France (6, 5)
15 One man's meat is another man's hat-band? (9)
16 Ground facility to aid flier in difficulties (8)
18 Army man's land register (7)
19 Confiscate Ezra's statement of identity . . . (7)
20 . . . or the source of Animal Farm, so called (6)
22 Like dissenters for the present occasion (5)
25 Addition to the family calls for a drink (3)

22

Across

1 Equal financial reward when novice enters golf competition (5, 4)
6 Girl on the piano – capital in Mediterranean island (5)
9 Most kindred are in the home (7)
10 Number I and several more find offensive (7)
11 Appropriate ceremonial form in speech (5)
12 Italian wine – not an unusual surprise (3, 2, 4)
13 Fat and wet (8)
15 Sounds so disgusted (4)
19 One still is first to make a snow man (4)
20 17th century girl straddles a horse (8)
23 Horror of man beset by weird spectre (3, 6)
24 Fish – one caught inside grounds (5)
26 'In general' (I quote) 'That divides exactly' (7)
27 Palm-oil left out of bilberry pie (7)
28 Twisted, without head or arms (5)
29 Never mourn about one gone but not forgotten (9)

Down

1 Dogsbody may find a new position about 11 (3, 6)
2 In a nasal tone they announce 'A meal – eat up' (5)
3 They don't get drunk, although let loose among plenty (8)
4 In general, cards are much less (3, 5)
5 One who is drawn from New England? (6)
6 In a factory one is easily modified (6)
7 Hurry up and give ring to destructive female in love (4, 5)
8 A small section, but proficient (5)
14 Huntsmen are very fit (2, 3, 4)
16 Place card has Christopher and two more names (5, 4)
17 Dad's skin is fairly good (8)
18 Doing repairs – it's work at last (8)
21 A cycle is available (6)
22 Kind of maggot (6)
23 Mark two (5)
25 Kid influenced by speech (5)

23

Across

1 E Anglian lakes order a cutter (10)
6 Drop it by order (4)
9 He tries to give old priests free treats (10)
10 Archduke, for one, brings forward end of disturbance (4)
12 Habit not normally in evidence, supporting duds? (12)
15 Student member in a tipsy state after pass (9)
17 Excursion for everyone within the bounds of Surrey (5)
18 Reputation of circle displaying 19 (5)
19 Severity new in a novelist's son (9)
20 One generally introduced to get rid of ill feeling? (12)
24 Bird one's following in the same passage (4)
25 He provides for strikers and seeks to form a union (10)
26 Producer of lava and, in France, sodium (4)
27 Underground dwarfs heard marking time? (10)

Down

1 Rustic's family deserts him – what a blow! (4)
2 An operatic hero lost his head in this bacchanal (4)
3 In staged rite, characters lose cohesion (12)
4 Comparatively bad areas – Dyfed or Kent, perhaps? (5)
5 Reserve one in Reformed Church centre (9)
7 Court in which mother is promised a view, say? (10)
8 Revolutionary movement with highest attainment level is Continental . . . (10)
11 . . . like this person, do we assume, relatively speaking? (6-6)
13 Many a short contest held by Miss Liddell's partner (10)
14 Assignment left in a particular spot (10)
16 Never satisfied, Titania's changed direction (9)
21 Happen to recognize officer with dog (5)
22 Read quickly through second Kipling novel (4)
23 King Edward thus erected his statue in London (4)

24

Across

1 Throw in a diamond (5)
4 It provides blanket coverage – for dorm feast? (9)
9 Poet involved with fruit cake (5, 4)
10 Trade union in current stoppage, in fact (5)
11 Cider-drinker or wine type I included (5)
12 Dives for coins a great deal (5-4)
13 Apart from Roman coin below (7)
15 Is this disease a type of shingles, almost? (7)
18 Making do? Maybe that conceals our state (7)
20 23's blazer has one in support (7)
21 Opening lots of letters, they may share our secrets (9)
23 Drag behind rear section? That's about right (5)
25 Stage part Adam created for himself (5)
26 A national disaster for a Turk (9)
27 Preservative makes Jack safe, we hear (9)
28 This emperor sometimes got drunk (5)

Down

1 Publication where you'll find daily puzzle (9)
2 He turns up set of clothes, including type of shirt (5)
3 Having loaf on fire is so rash (3-6)
4 Rose, perhaps, or Amelia (7)
5 Get order confused and explode grenade (7)
6 Field for fair person (according to Johnson) (5)
7 Surrender to another country (9)
8 French writer in Russian councils (5)
14 Forced flat, perhaps? (9)
16 Ridley's train won't pull out – the place is deserted (5, 4)
17 Commiseration for players' difficulty (4, 5)
19 Like ill-disposed characters (7)
20 Crossing the channel (7)
21 Such an informer may be bent (5)
22 Snap – or nip? (3-2)
24 Reproducing a bullet's sound (5)

25

Across

1 Give warning of harbour limit (7)
5 What an alarming blood count! (7)
9 Pair take in champion horse (5)
10 Deliverance of the army so valiant and free (9)
11 Concentration of high tars? (9)
12 Male voice, noiseless in Stoke Poges (5)
13 Members' divisions brought up at party meetings (5)
15 Corinthian letter-opener (9)
18 Religious state doing less reconstruction (9)
19 Tendency of old penny to chink (5)
21 Topping stuff for severe cold symptoms (5)
23 Sage round a ham – with Irish stew? (9)
25 The Camptown tower has a knocker (9)
26 Eccentric cheer-leader at head of column (5)
27 Balance to settle around the fourth of January (7)
28 Cape bird is trapped in reservoir (7)

Down

1 Some cheering at this address? (3-4)
2 Split about how French counsel should appear (9)
3 Wrong source of Shakespearian comedy (5)
4 Pique and complaint about heartless pal (9)
5 Attractive girl easily caught in the field (5)
6 Policy of keeping people isolated, hide being different (9)
7 A charge after a French wedding (5)
8 Course for those wishing to take the chair, say (7)
14 Some protection in Rugby Union, dashing all over the place (4-5)
16 Sort of ropy dish, set before crowned head, makes him so uneasy (9)
17 Trim scaphoid (9)
18 Youth leader accepts pound in foreign money (7)
20 Plot may do this to clot (7)
22 Stress of 23 *dn* in strict usage (5)
23 Unit of length settled by soldiers (5)
24 Stands tortures (5)

26

Across

1 Artisan whose work caused feathers to fly (8)
5 Composer of fine lines in order to eat (6)
10 An offer of equality in race matters? (5)
11 On stage they can almost create phantasies (9)
12 Song catches on, supported by the ratings (5-4)
13 How to get a sovereign out of pawn (5)
14 Growing need for such accommodation (7)
16 Intense rivalry could be magnetic (6)
19 Takes steps to form a union (6)
21 Clear share of the profit (4-3)
23 Bones in a circle? (5)
25 Dining out with aunt we hear you left fuming (9)
27 Seat with four-legged support (9)
28 In principle give a vote to the island (5)
29 Stay in side-street after riot (6)
30 Difficult situations where direct strikes must be avoided (8)

Down

1 Author who might have made a slip? (8)
2 Of those entitled to make their mark (9)
3 Type of job for copper to start (5)
4 It may be true, say, the flower gets more water here (7)
6 Two noises not amounting to much (9)
7 Famous bowler making a duck (5)
8 Error in dress becoming apparent (6)
9 Hold Horatio on the bridge? (6)
15 The monster must have gone, say, for vacation (9)
17 Double act? (4-5)
18 Frequently out of date (3-5)
20 Not a straightforward sort of flight (6)
21 Characteristic of the brave (7)
22 Flower identified by spider and bee (6)
24 One member of the Beetles a girl? (5)
26 Part of Antigua noted for fertiliser production (5)

27

1 Norm remits rent to his mate (7)
5 What's to be done when a king gets on his hind legs . . . (7)
9 . . . and holds the French to be less formal? (5)
10 Seneca one of this brave family (9)
11 Failure to notice surveillance (9)
12 Dolly's musical greeting (5)
13 Authorisation here to reverse the hour glass (5)
15 Not recognised, having no precedent (7-2)
18 He controls the movements of the little people (9)
19 Stitches causing strain, we hear (5)
21 Made an example of depressed characters (5)
23 Turn angry, having first tried the food (9)
25 A broomstick is misused by women (9)
26 Thrust from air intake an eye-opener (5)
27 Sum for patentee of sovereign remedy? (7)
28 Relinquish a position in home for alcoholics (7)

Down

1 Where to sit when milking cows (7)
2 Chart useful at Mafeking (6, 3)
3 Clumsy Saxon bearing operatic heroine here (5)
4 Measuring device for cats and dogs (4-6)
5 A division of the Yard is moving (5)
6 Disorderly actors are plastered (9)
7 King in Elia's characters from Shakespeare? No, Duke's servant (5)
8 What to do when a player offends badly (4, 3)
14 Monotonous routine in prison (9)
16 Marx perhaps, Nero maybe, Queequeg certainly (9)
17 The decline of exotic rhythm (9)
18 Chukka, say, involving this player (7)
20 Overindulge in a salad of Oriental fruits (7)
22 Greedy kind of bank, this (5)
23 Sort of field familiar to an Irishman (5)
24 Red Sea opening for the Israelites (5)

28

Across

1 The eccentric gave a car next – such prodigality! (12)
8 Get some benefit from a noble deed (7)
9 Workers absorbing article about a star (7)
11 Choosy individual with a marked preference (7)
12 One is made to accept an order that's offensive (7)
13 The fighting man's face-saving device (5)
14 Transport for those wanting personal attention (9)
16 Aim to include every form of hesitation and disloyalty (9)
19 It's light to carry (5)
21 Applied decoration to finished poem (7)
23 Left with original backing – swell! (4, 3)
24 No conscientious guy needs to hurry (7)
25 Some people seethe at repellent plays (7)
26 Seeing Roman rotters misbehaving, he made complaint (12)

Down

1 Quick to get out of jam (7)
2 A supporter of the pig and pony (7)
3 Take turns later maybe – neat solution (9)
4 Making a return once more (5)
5 Crowded dwelling for six-footers (3-4)
6 Duck boxed in picture (7)
7 Bookings made with certain misgivings (12)
10 He gives a moving performance in 25 (5-7)
15 Where horses are given a drink in town (9)
17 Cheer for most of the players at end of game (7)
18 Coy pals' drunken song (7)
19 The sunburned man's touching line (7)
20 A roll containing nothing but chicken (7)
22 Speak up about sailors' stories (5)

29

Across

1 Redcap in trouble with lousy mount (7)
5 Series of eight months full of hail (7)
9 Discard manual holder for cuttings (9)
10 An extremist, when he gets jolly blue (5)
11 Too weak to produce loud abuse? (5)
12 Disputed inheritance held up by Freeman (9)
14 Survey shows the fiddle has a place in artistic revival (14)
17 Raking in great fees for minister's perk (6, 8)
21 Galen worked in his part of the world for relief of discomfort (9)
23 Legend about the Black Mountain of Africa (5)
24 Finnish author (5)
25 As worn by the Hound of Heaven? (3-6)
26 Our queen is having a baby, can't keep quiet (7)
27 Crafty directors, it's right they should be milked (7)

Down

1 It's not all loss, if you become callous (6)
2 Distance gained by the police on *The Times* (7)
3 Head swallows the tablet – no frills (9)
4 This generation is acting without any prompting (11)
5 A satisfactory outcome, would you call it? (3)
6 One of a handy pair (5)
7 T. A. never changed this old soldier (7)
8 Masefield's main complaint (3-5)
13 Exciting serial – The Sword under the Rock (5-6)
15 Not where the Bard lived in London (9)
16 Tucking into venison, is unable to be the wine-pourer (8)
18 Gibbon composed poetry about Jehovah (7)
19 Sadly unable to get over the English mists (7)
20 Do all this team get the red card? (6)
22 He started a row in the barrack-room (5)
25 Stop that girl! (3)

30

Across

1 Some gamble, how a ship may react to rough seas, say (5-3-4)
9 His journey to a star United Nations organized (9)
10 One French boy or girl in dire need (5)
11 Somebody's depression a jolly introduction to hell? (6)
12 River Arrow's engine part (8)
13 Pipe for a rugby player, say? (6)
15 Like Ketèlbey's garden showing no return in gum resin (8)
18 Sweet dog Bill Sikes owned (5-3)
19 A black queen first in her order (6)
21 This well shows how Descartes' follower lost his head (8)
23 Endured, say, by company that goes to the wall (6)
26 Synonym or antonym of 'fast'? (5)
27 Unusually long title to describe 'The Wages of Sin' (3-6)
28 Abandon one's country to live in seclusion here? (6, 6)

Down

1 Old Egyptian gambling game, it's said (7)
2 One of those up the pole (add 'em up) (5)
3 Ruffians teasing a lion? Gosh! (9)
4 With this early navigator at last 13 becomes a pirate (4)
5 Greek-style quadruped to depart in confusion (8)
6 Cantonese however is not their regional dialect (5)
7 Disheartened trapper upset with ease, say, by this comeback (8)
8 Scottish footballers appear kind of cross (6)
14 Offering to withdraw one thousand dollars from contract (8)
16 A pound on at Wyeville for one to beat the Eagle (9)
17 Bestiary is rewritten by a voluptuary (8)
18 Darwin's ocean-going hound (6)
20 Was contemptuous of the second sort of beef (7)
22 Took legal proceedings over English kid (5)
24 Ask for a pin for this surplice (5)
25 Secret plan to put money in the kitty (4)

31

Across

1 Drug bar at wild party for Indians (8)
5 Rarely producing new models (6)
10 Right filling for tooth, one sort of canine (5)
11 State of some Americans just off the Needles? (3, 6)
12 Desolate region explored by Eliot (5, 4)
13 Crowd in Channel port moving right to left (5)
14 Room for audience for this sort of music (7)
16 Inform of tiny adjustment (6)
19 Old saw that's lost its cutting edge (6)
21 Diet rich enough for so-called film star? (7)
23 Blackbirds in woods, for example (5)
25 Villainous crimes upset social worker (9)
27 Letter or card (9)
28 Essential for a showgirl with no capital left (5)
29 More down South, summer's not so sunny (6)
30 Butter more evenly spread to fry at the end (8)

Down

1 Clubman's quick rhymes (8)
2 Depends on follower for runs (5, 4)
3 Quick article, as it happens (5)
4 Stars horseman, so to speak (7)
6 One who improves parts of Notre Dame (9)
7 Circular objects in place of entertainment (5)
8 Disorder for a month on the border (6)
9 Editor's put in news that's upset this country (6)
15 Cast off here for second part of journey (9)
17 Allowed, say, the part below the crust of this port (9)
18 Chaps keep score in mind (8)
20 Opposition makes two points in my case it appears (6)
21 Kind of valve in heart gets second wind (7)
22 Airman in a kite can be counted on (6)
24 Said to apply in this part of South-East (5)
26 Strive to fix immovably inside (5)

31

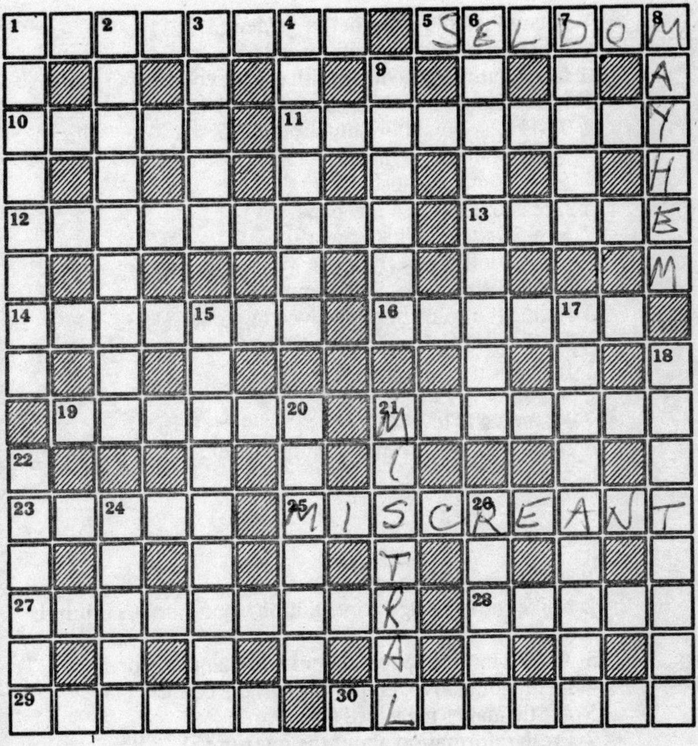

This puzzle was completed within 30 minutes by 26 per cent of the competitors at the 1986 London B regional final of the Times Collins Dictionaries Crossword Championship.

32

Across

1 A comfortable place in the garden (3, 2, 5)
6 Old part of Swanage destroyed (4)
10 Chocolate cake to have with cheese covering (7)
11 Make more records from master (7)
12 Tell tales, say, about my superior (5, 4)
13 Wander about in the mountains (5)
14 Board sends English doctor to America (5)
15 Occasionally see a few papers (9)
17 Saw Sweden – it's stirring (9)
20 What's left of the river (5)
21 The latest in style, Sally's outfit (5)
23 Fixing the value of grass given to donkeys (9)
25 Instructed trade union to see the German revolutionary (7)
26 An error in 1 *ac* (7)
27 Plane is still level (4)
28 Mountain crest comprises hog's-back shape (10)

Down

1 Ruth left a noisy scene (5)
2 Make the expected contribution when Lorna's injured (2, 4, 3)
3 After a motion, peers defer kin's claim to property (7, 7)
4 Demanding love, emperor leads the country (7)
5 A title makes me a lord (7)
7 Fresh information about the interior (5)
8 Spread spare lids out (9)
9 Theatre – of war? (10, 4)
14 Obtainable from there, a new girdle (9)
16 Street-vendor makin' a mess of island (6-3)
18 Con man turns up in disgrace (7)
19 Refuse to go in here and clean tip up (7)
22 In Paris, a match is free (5)
24 Eat too much Cheddar, perhaps (5)

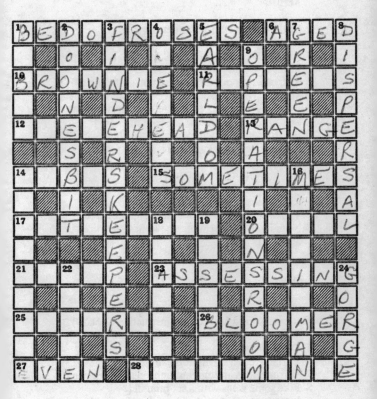

¹B	E	D	O	³F	R	⁴O	S	⁵E	S		⁶A	⁷G	E	⁸D
		O		I				A		⁹O		R		I
¹⁰B	R	O	W	N	I	E		¹¹R		P	E	E		S
		N		D				L		E	E			P
¹²		E		E	H	E	A	D		¹³R	A	N	G	E
		S		R				O		A				R
¹⁴		B		S		¹⁵S	O	M	E	T	I	M	E	S
		I		K						I			¹⁶	A
¹⁷		T	E		¹⁸	¹⁹	²⁰O			O	N			L
		E					O			N				
²¹		²²P			²³A	S	S	E	S	S	I	N	G	²⁴
		E					R			R				O
²⁵		R				²⁶B	L	O	O	M	E	R		G
		S					O			O		A		E
²⁷V	E	N		²⁸			M			N		N		E

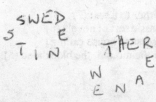

KINSPEER
S
REFED

SWED
S   E
  TIN   THERE
      W A
      E N

33

Across

1 Bottom team after defender (8)
5 Cat's-cradle land? (6)
10 In a bad way, get NHS trial done (2, 3, 6, 4)
11 Fire bar an old piece of brass (7)
12 You can't get out if these are not kept open (7)
13 Suspicion of corrosion after condensation (8)
15 Butterfly – one of a pair often seen upside down (5)
18 See 'ere, I say, window does not open! (5)
20 Potatoes in this style expected to include game? (8)
23 Place in Regent's Park, perhaps, for Oscar Wilde in 'The Sea Goose'? (7)
25 Brighten No 10 for so long (7)
26 Was it sworn at Versailles in a tie-break situation? (6-5, 4)
27 The old sign of those not quite gentlemen (6)
28 Notedly theatrical Scotch governor embraces English artist (8)

Down

1 Casually raise the volume? (6)
2 It comes from Mecca, this instruction book (9)
3 Water ice, a bit of a refresher between times (7)
4 Draw cheque (5)
6 Variable pitch up in Morecambe (7)
7 Surreptitious attempt announced in Irish town (5)
8 Like some wells with a set rainfall (8)
9 In matters spiritual, he is coasting freely (8)
14 Play without stress? (8)
16 Villain's violent crimes against a worker (9)
17 Thick woods always used for bow-mast support (8)
19 Redskin's whip? (7)
21 One who helps another to a seat (7)
22 Obsessed by this classic sort of novel? (6)
24 People look down on such house-calling (5)
25 Climber's first over the mound, the blockhead (5)

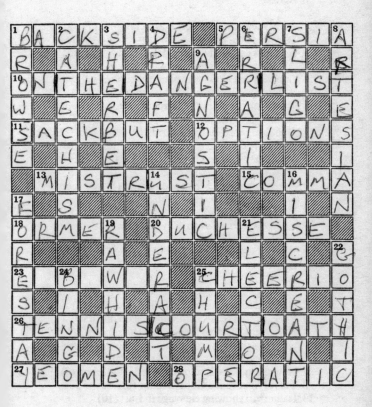

34

Across

1 After the show, dash back for a fastener (7)
5 What republicans hope to do for a career? (7)
9 A number acting rejected this smaller group (5)
10 About time to change this navigational aid! (9)
11 Care about a backward plant (6)
12 Abandoned crew said to have blasphemed (8)
14 Greybeard, a military man at heart (5)
15 Limit vote somehow? It's a recurring theme (9)
18 Queen entered club restaurant (9)
20 One's sweetheart may be so old-fashioned (5)
22 Court Deputy Lieutenant – also cops, say? (8)
24 Look in to criticize the race (6)
26 Native beheaded Maori, being wild (9)
27 Order observed in 16, I confess (5)
28 He embraced a girl – from Thessaly, perhaps (7)
29 Young Isambard's territory (7)

Down

1 Source of sweetness hard to come by on manoeuvres (9)
2 Disregarded rising soldier, a Right-winger (7)
3 Benefactress heads south or goes up north in it (9)
4 Arkwright's lack of response in the surgery? (4)
5 Clean up the musical? It takes the biscuit (4, 6)
6 Identifies fellow upset over art in France (5)
7 New trio in East End providing the antiphon (7)
8 Travel right to the Kent area for furs, say (5)
13 Italian girl showing cleavage in East (10)
16 In the sea, everyone has one on for decoration (9)
17 A companion one has in one's pocket (4-5)
19 Cutter many'll say is at home in a Mexican lake (7)
21 Like vultures, only found in the borders of Thailand (7)
22 A ghost one exorcised in anger (5)
23 Collective knowledge about 27's first French department (5)
25 Bill is a schoolmaster (4)

35

Across

1 Twin found gold (6)
4 Beetle's penalty for too much indulgence? (8)
10 Dramatist is one who wrote Utopia without fabrication (7)
11 Wild animal once of the bovine or such a variety (7)
12 As a diplomat he appears in capital form (10)
13 Go for a short walk (4)
15 Keep saying it was, classically, the origin of earth (7)
17 Was this smoker more healthy in the first place? (7)
19 To prepare for execution may so occupy a law clerk's attention (7)
21 Hardy lass has time for a bit of mosaic work (7)
23 Is it hard for the creditor to get? (4)
24 Sugar-loaf unobtainable at the confectioner's (10)
27 His invention was instrumental in Crippen's capture (7)
28 Sweet little couple having a row (7)
29 Supporter or representative of modern monarchy (8)
30 Dreads squirming poisonous creatures (6)

Down

1 Tom's high-rise accommodation in tents on a river (9)
2 Like this clue describing eg sugar in tea? (7)
3 Eclipse – how he used to dominate the field? (10)
5 Dramatic title role – a customer for Burke and Hare (9)
6 Trick put up to get round the credit-transfer system (4)
7 Supply with provisions cut in pieces in a small bottle (7)
8 Pine extract engineer found over the wilderness (5)
9 Deal arranged by 1 *ac's* mother (4)
14 On which Alice won her promotion (10)
16 Former adaptation of Welsh rite (9)
18 Comply with request to forward study outfit (9)
20 Chemical warfare ploy said to be affecting the inner man (7)
22 In mid-week send for the recluse (7)
23 Milton's work, sounds like 'The Shaggy Dogs' Plea' (5)
25 Remark especially – ie call out (4)
26 Game with northern diving bird (4)

36

Across

1 A barbarous language, the Pomeranian tongue? (3, 5)
5 Party meeting when out of range of Russia (6)
10 Problem area of blacks and whites here (9, 6)
11 Small loopholes in regard to permits (7)
12 Extras helping to gladden Darby and Joan (7)
13 Always included in a stage direction (8)
15 More than one spoke, coming out of the centre (5)
18 Sound circuit's failure (5)
20 In this mood you can make your choice (8)
23 Fish allowed as a delicacy for tea (7)
25 The office representative admitted to Christian name (7)
26 This pop hysteria is strange for a manual health worker (15)
27 Dashing, like a ship built for speed (6)
28 Kaleidoscopic light may be irresistible (8)

Down

1 Richard and King Edward haggle (6)
2 March stiffly to iron part of staircase (5, 4)
3 Perhaps a Sûreté stiff? (7)
4 Jives, say, in clubs (5)
6 Apart when asleep (7)
7 Behave deceitfully to relative, we hear (5)
8 Name Cesario concealed in the plot (8)
9 CO's assistant has one no-trump? He'll be lying next! (8)
14 Deserter gets place in a crew by word of mouth (8)
16 Angler, or his prey (5-4)
17 House buzzer may be stuck on here (3-5)
19 Somehow Alice's grabbed the right cakes (7)
21 Two boys, one in the percussion section (7)
22 Easy to get annoyed (6)
24 Canoe plying to and fro (5)
25 What's in this container may be boiled in kettle (5)

37

Across

1 Remove foil and allay suspicion (6)
5 Well-known climber, I scale Mt Tumbledown (8)
9 I stand corrected, in front of church, for aloofness (8)
10 Tired agent taking shelter inside (6)
11 Duffer's on the organ – better wear these! (3-5)
12 This nurse a valiant leader in dungeon (6)
13 Variegated star does break up (8)
15 Knockdown said to be fatal (4)
17 Cries of distress or just one about Beachy Head? (4)
19 Nick shows how goose is cooked (8)
20 Restore retired premier to state (6)
21 Walpole's ability to strike lucky banishes depression in peace (8)
22 Guard transported by rail (6)
23 Don, for example, is so impractical (8)
24 First of eleven players in Orient has right of way (8)
25 A fair vehicle but over-powered (6)

Down

2 Limit a bleeper – part can be taken off (8)
3 Withering, like Shelley's deep tone (8)
4 Show ring and give promises of party (9)
5 Where striker stands defiant, not easily ruffled (6-9)
6 Duck-doctor takes all morning to go round (7)
7 14th century appears modern in outskirts of Torino (8)
8 Does an agent put it into orbit? (8)
14 Bedeck a king in this demi-paradise (9)
15 Just lies sprawled out in a kind of sweater (4, 4)
16 Crumbs! Svengali has gone mad (8)
17 Pen-pusher – possibly a royal official (8)
18 Straddle top mount (8)
19 How monotonous to sing wordlessly with regular beat (7)

38

Across

1 Home Guard (5-3)
9 Publicize ship or plane (8)
10 Choice of directions exhausted (4)
11 Painstaking passenger in the way (12)
13 Projecting place (6)
14 Creature caught in delicate trap, oddly (8)
15 Main wine, such as Bordeaux (7)
16 China not the origin of this sort of garden (7)
20 Endures a disaster in submarine (8)
22 Scene rewritten by a dramatist (6)
23 Moderate policy contributing to 3? (6, 6)
25 His vessel had a full complement of mates (4)
26 It's put on bit by bit (3-5)
27 League members seen at ends of some matches (8)

Down

2 Write off in a recess (8)
3 Sort of recent feast facing pages inside (6, 6)
4 Carefree social beginner once, broadcasting (8)
5 About five, somehow get to a dance (7)
6 Grotesque person as leader of French side (6)
7 Girl's name appearing in articles (4)
8 Warm as some Pacific islands (8)
12 Open to make one see red resin (12)
15 Ideal partner – for monogamist, we hear (4, 4)
17 Said to be celebrated (8)
18 This programme gives the running order, of course (8)
19 Hard to get some deliveries into royal house (7)
21 Vegetable associated with North Country (6)
24 Desert? Not a lot of water (4)

This was the 1987 Qualifying puzzle for the Times Collins Dictionaries Crossword Championship.

39

Across

1 Drink brought back by mother from holiday resort (5)
4 Reformed lags swear anyone can see through this (9)
9 A home should include quarters for wood (3, 6)
10 Advert about iron, right? (5)
11 Lend a certain sparkle (6)
12 Esoteric drink to encourage (8)
14 Taking new help on, mean to produce miraculous result (10)
16 Suspend for quite a mild imprecation (4)
19 Forced to return the cheese (4)
20 Russian capitalists! (10)
22 Footballer behaving like a baby? (8)
23 Twist a guy after a court order (6)
26 Pole in space – a scene of much action (5)
27 Like list to include really good aggressive man (9)
28 Settles as arranged for flat (9)
29 Engineers with hoist take a turn running water (5)

Down

1 Make a bomb from fruit under tree (9)
2 Scowl when let down (5)
3 Notice works getting into shape for a take-over (8)
4 A song can give great pleasure (4)
5 Mid-morning Daniel goes to church gate (10)
6 Fights waste (6)
7 A key company worker is one who stands by his word (9)
8 Bird in regrettable condition (5)
13 Turn the corner and create pure chaos (10)
15 Questioning people (9)
17 Cut before the consumer can get warmer (3-6)
18 A form giving rise to extreme dislike (8)
21 Dedicated old boy no longer alive (6)
22 Drawing many a primitive means of transport (5)
24 Pluck is called for to make such a sound (5)
25 As one's written repeatedly, she was highly respected (4)

40

Across

1 I heal a bitter rift and restore name (12)
9 Sweet Dickensian do-gooder catches bachelor (5, 4)
10 Pooh's young friend accepts me as a lover (5)
11 Doctor called according to the rota (6)
12 Drab is a false label for this Shakespearian heroine (8)
13 Privileged admission to course (6)
15 Mastering it may need solid study (8)
18 His country's defeat means nothing to Russian composer (8)
19 Notice a gap coming (6)
21 He made himself a butt of cynicism (8)
23 Naturally cold state, but sweet when baked (6)
26 It may be forced to obtain a decision (5)
27 Australian town boy can explain his selection, naturally (9)
28 How Jaques might think the whole world was organised? (5-7)

Down

1 Show delight about novelist's talk (7)
2 Mercury he noted: boiling outside, start of lovely summer (5)
3 Who takes her to the musical? (9)
4 Not quite the female a herdsman expected (4)
5 Hey! Tests somehow reveal he ate his own children (8)
6 Painful reminder of passion when taken to heart (5)
7 No tussle about a race course here (8)
8 Bay, for example, is certainly one of its objects of study (6)
14 He taught the Mock Turtle (obviously he had his own house) (8)
16 Helping of beef, perhaps, from prize animal (9)
17 David, for example, has inferior act to Goliath – to start with (8)
18 Such a means to an end barely contemplated by Dane (6)
20 Practised diner at buffet (7)
22 Saints choose to be beheaded (5)

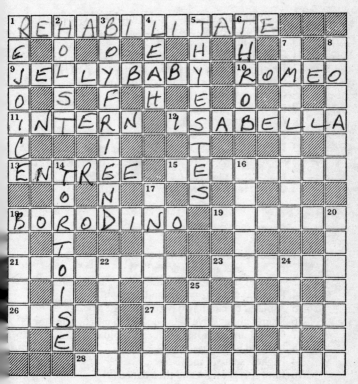

HEYS
TEST

24 Jazz or rock? (5)
25 A curious flower (4)

41

Across

1 Outlying part of Eden – or Hampstead? (6, 6)
9 Following saying . . . (9)
10 . . . is a maxim for a dwarf (5)
11 Study intently for every purpose (6)
12 Reigning beauty in a hat is unfairly satirised (8)
13 Item set apart for special service (6)
15 Certainly in drink, but restrained (8)
18 Born writer finishes with the drug (8)
19 Ground down by some Herod edict (6)
21 Pots needed for cold part of the garden (8)
23 Laborious tasks for the wife in country mansions (6)
26 Secretary takes care of a painting on dry plaster (5)
27 Match rose material for front of dress (9)
28 Carrier for a pusher (12)

Down

1 Classified as 'U' – felt in the dark about it (7)
2 He who gets up to go down? (5)
3 As an example seniors may be going forth (9)
4 Reputed to be heavy around one (4)
5 Amused by cunning devices in a plot (8)
6 Regret about drive being up due to mischief-maker (5)
7 Caught unconscious about real trouble (8)
8 Inclined to be guarded (6)
14 Highest score? Fine (3-5)
16 Idiot – to get tight and then dance (9)
17 Capacity to inspire followers in a march is unusual (8)
18 One Conservative in residence is very particular (6)
20 Edward comes up bothering 2 – he wants something (7)
22 Two kings – one makes money abroad (5)
24 A good man about – he wins the plate (5)
25 A divided populace in a biblical land (4)

42

Across

1 Strip-joints opening today (6)
4 Travelling-clock? (8)
10 Country home of three belles we hear (9)
11 Bellini's work has the usual cut (5)
12 Let's change to nothing short of mineral water (7)
13 Charge for keeping goods and silver in warehouse (7)
14 Sell the dummy – touchdown possible (3, 2)
15 Fag-end got bent in picking up the pieces (8)
18 Pair in light kiss and cuddle (8)
20 Is 'A' so out of tune we need a musical alternative? (5)
23 Mount that is dangerous when active . . . (7)
25 . . . abusing fence, perhaps (7)
26 Cold store base (5)
27 The unenlightened inflame Professor Higgins (9)
28 Serving as guardian yet ultra-changeable (8)
29 Damage to church is seldom met with (6)

Down

1 Down payments for measures of coal, for example (8)
2 French verse form broadcast after six (7)
3 By writing this, zoo can be made so – with sudden emphasis (9)
5 Gear-changing practice for road show? (5, 9)
6 Chap to travel for tropical fruit (5)
7 Ground where there is no parking for a water-tortoise (7)
8 Standard text-book for a senior lecturer (6)
9 Perhaps the good marry if she waves her wand (5, 9)
16 Strange one brightened this classical old age (9)
17 One is set to drain off water when royal egg is cooked (8)
19 Railmen taking part in minor complaint (7)
21 Flight engineer concerned with pitch? (7)
22 This wader has an octave range (6)
24 Shock for a Scandinavian mountaineer (5)

43

Across

1 Hat giving protection in nursery (6)
4 Understood 13 beheaded in accordance with the law (8)
10 Nervously tense, like a rider when drunk (7)
11 Betray everyone in this boat (7)
12 Ulster may depend on one (4-6)
13 Trimming a couple of army men (4)
15 Play in afternoon with new England opener in team (7)
17 Half-baked pudding is hard (7)
19 Gets inside information in return for savings (4, 3)
21 Boy holds sort of yarn or rope for fastening (7)
23 Heartlessness, perhaps? Nothing in it (4)
24 Right group gets card early in week (6, 4)
27 Declines part of Arab (7)
28 Hear out novel writer (7)
29 She lets country boy away, finally (8)
30 How do we stand one? (6)

Down

1 Prior, Swift and Pope, for example (9)
2 Survive in first? (7)
3 Overbearing as victim of hold-up? (4-6)
5 Self-willed maiden creates a fluster (9)
6 Idle head (4)
7 Goldsmith joining small group in Irish capital (7)
8 Fill pot (3, 2)
9 This college sent down no odd characters, however (4)
14 Time launch round day's end in part of Ireland (6, 4)
16 Absorbed what's writ large (9)
18 Conceal spring that's narrow and rigid (9)
20 Half-prepared to make big strides in Cambridgeshire (7)
22 Complaint porter intended to be heard (7)
23 For example, a volume about partners (5)
25 Fruit a number of Romans consumed (4)
26 Man's place as PM once (4)

44

Across

1 The Army's domestic task force? (7-5)
9 One male ideal that is not fully realized (9)
10 Return a cycle to the sports ground (5)
11 Rachel's little boy catching lake fish (6)
12 No point knocking here – the tradesman's entrance is free (4, 4)
13 Optical shutter (6)
15 Mishit an error in these games (8)
18 Inadequate parking – he's in the top storey (8)
19 Don't start to criticise the fire-water! (6)
21 Short passage from satirist about a schoolboy (8)
23 Left in peace, say, he is full of joy (6)
26 Provide food in battered crate (5)
27 Silas in G & S version used to make jellies (9)
28 Author's contraction avoided in typing (7, 5)

Down

1 Easy to make crumble – can be cooked in fat? (7)
2 Peg to hold opera hat (5)
3 Diverge, oddly, about a French verbal adjective (9)
4 Old wives' kisses, say (4)
5 Sort of betting before and after the event in Rome (4-4)
6 School crocodile (5)
7 Girl admits forged coin is a plant (8)
8 Restaurant proprietor who might give someone a living (6)
14 The total number of sappers in existence (8)
16 Church girl rings thrice – a variation of telling the hours (9)
17 1000 to one race is an error (8)
18 With father, the beginning and end of charity is a religious organisation (6)
20 Lively party, where Mrs Brown was invited to dance? (5-2)
22 He has the remedy for a smoker (5)
24 *In absentia*, ranked as top band (5)
25 This is the platform for departures, the porter said (4)

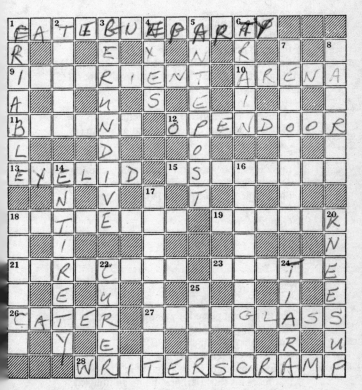

This puzzle, used as a tie-breaker in the Birmingham regional final of the Times Collins Dictionaries Crossword Championship, was solved by the winner in 16 minutes.

45

Across

1 Dance in prison (5)
4 Settle sectarian differences (9)
9 Baseball player taking time-out (9)
10 Lawrence with the Japanese sash he washes (5)
11 Many wrong retreating but victorious general (5)
12 To sum up, 10 empties to be collected (9)
13 Economise in vain (7)
15 Head not shown in attractive picture (7)
18 Mother's unusual means of keeping warm (7)
20 Joint medical speciality that's brilliant (7)
21 Supports archbishop, in a manner of speaking (4, 5)
23 In Slough, starts to utter specie that's counterfeit (5)
25 Turn back if the experiment is dubious (5)
26 Flower pictures I suppress (9)
27 Cut obsolescent fuel store (9)
28 Gambling row (5)

Down

1 Counsel to reform and stop recording (4, 5)
2 7-1 – walk-over (5)
3 Getting warm place for gymnastic exercises (2, 3, 4)
4 Bill Lock, one in play (7)
5 Put top on glue – it's upset (7)
6 Show travelled round (5)
7 Oldest inhabitant from a source in Lincoln . . . (9)
8 . . . loses his shirt perhaps, being gullible (5)
14 Makes proper use of taxes the sovereign introduced (9)
16 Replies conversely 'Go forwards' (4-5)
17 Persuaded great PM to climb up and drop off (2, 2, 5)
19 Around Dover, prize appears offshore (7)
20 The girl has changed, having lost weight (7)
21 Muddle up fare some days (5)
22 Authority keeps mum (3-2)
24 Simpleton employed by a tailor (5)

45

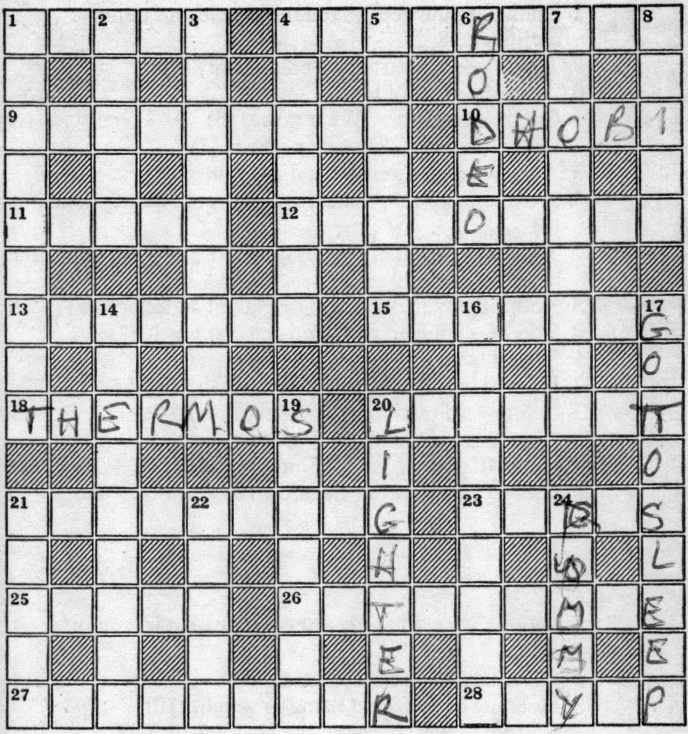

46

Across

1 Epithalamium gets a similar green sort of union certificate (8, 5)
9 Toady's refusal to accept edited copy (9)
10 A bit of a show of temperament? (5)
11 Cut by the skipper? What sauce! (5)
12 Denry Machin's diamond perhaps (4)
13 A hankering to join the Italian Church (4)
15 See doctor about pressure from this old money-lender (7)
17 To whom his father relates difficulties of borrowing and lending (7)
18 Nothing turned out about origin of Chinese print (7)
20 50% of school get wretched zero for music (7)
21 Slough farm building perhaps (4)
22 Mineral extracted from metal containers (4)
23 Psalmist's direction put an end to 14 (5)
26 Able to return to where Napoleon suffered it (5)
27 A sort of pigeon dance? Some game! (9)
28 Poet so hammers out transformations (13)

Down

1 Show, with grand girls, otherwise called Harmonica (7, 7)
2 Summarize 11's revised version (5)
3 Meaning one without name or weight (10)
4 Bottom of bag cut open – had a quick look (7)
5 Word for word it's the compositor's fault (7)
6 Is said to be acquainted with an informer (4)
7 How Addison described himself in this periodical (9)
8 Fiend in one of his 28, see – help stop him (14)
14 Extremely aged man shows a lot of bottle (10)
16 Peculiar behaviour in an old art style (9)
19 A beam of light over the door (7)
20 Help shoot a gull, say (7)
24 Goes ahead with the roof-covering (5)
25 Sound measures of support for this achievement (4)

47

Across

1 Punish the wretched bard discovering this American songster! (12)
8 Horse and carriage? (7)
9 Pair to stage dance (3-4)
11 Damp mines to be modified (7)
12 Settle score (7)
13 Sorcerer decapitated mountain goat (5)
14 Those against being sent on pop revival (9)
16 One on top in some vulgar part (9)
19 Thus diluted beer is not drunk (5)
21 A few difficult to control (7)
23 Old ships out East making large amounts (7)
24 Two girls one on each knee (7)
25 Missile coming out of S African wood (7)
26 Intimate talk between a couple of cards (5, 2, 5)

Down

1 One I watch out for in Kansas (7)
2 Got a touch off by frenzied dieting (7)
3 Teaching a lesson in being generous (6, 3)
4 Work with credit say out of sight (5)
5 Feller like Davy Crockett (7)
6 Untie hair for wash-out (3-4)
7 Clearly a top-liner competition (12)
10 Fitting attire for high-flyers (8, 4)
15 Item – a capital plot (9)
17 He painted the heartless Dickensian doctor (7)
18 Monarch protects following pages from this bully (7)
19 Lassie and I rambling in Europe (7)
20 Delivered nothing by rail (7)
22 Nothing less will do? (5)

47

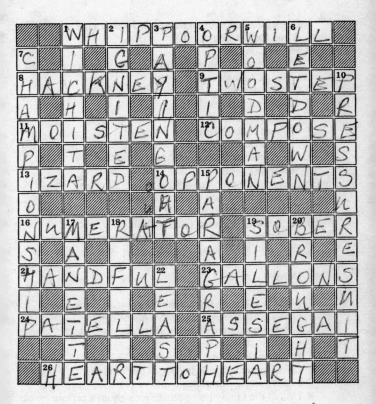

101

48

Across

1 Complaint made by well-qualified woman (6)
4 A job for the summer (8)
10 House rule (7)
11 Pleasant about rubbishy stuff, though it makes one blink (7)
12 Old driver seeing a fight in comfort (10)
13 Capital punishment! (4)
15 Annoyed, demanded to hold the money (7)
17 Striking entails disruption (7)
19 A key is held by the more morose cleaner (7)
21 Cheat – one with the wind up in America? (7)
23 Soft fish skin (4)
24 Little man is on time (6-4)
27 Keeping about fifty working like dogs (7)
28 A specimen is no longer big (7)
29 At the front, ordered into rear (8)
30 Parts always carried by a sea-going vessel (6)

Down

1 Physics, taken by those wishing to better themselves (9)
2 Orderly has to remain outside, it's ruled (7)
3 Where one should expect plenty of spirit from the workers (10)
5 Basis for the table d'hôte meal? (6-3)
6 Crawl in the fast lane in cheeky fashion (4)
7 Fancy getting one game in maybe (7)
8 One of the family being punctilious about a certain point (5)
9 This place is completely cut off, which makes the egghead play up (4)
14 '—him, I say, quite from your memory', said Mrs Malaprop (10)
16 It's desperate courage that makes many act about wrong-doing (7-2)
18 The exhausted feeling new residents can get (9)
20 Working round for a social worker (7)
22 A vagrant the French show no consideration for (7)
23 Manufactured food – finished article (5)

5 American newspaperman pressed into service (4)
6 Row about it in retirement (4)

49

Across

1 First-class airman's return to a European capital (5)
4 Abandoned type petting outside university (9)
9 Laboured vigorously at first, rebuilding a road (9)
10 Concern about Trotskyist beliefs (5)
11 Its contents are formed in a single layer (3-3)
12 The beast is about to catch Jeanie for one (8)
14 Tax botcher may be a blatherskite (10)
16 Predator in the sky plagues Kuala Lumpur (4)
19 Writer's his mock title (4)
20 Thoroughly modern girl grasps new term used in measurement (10)
22 Vestment they say you are wearing to marry (8)
23 This share gets several stars (6)
26 Declare perfect (5)
27 Fashionable French writer's second cloak (9)
28 Stop an order to persist in shelling (9)
29 Superior air adopted by society pages (5)

Down

1 Minister's company accepted by a superior (9)
2 Loud breather had a shy appearance (5)
3 Sufficient for a daughter to regard as similar (8)
4 Dull character on the staff (4)
5 Gangsters supporting our environment? (10)
6 Last month medical specialization appeared proper (6)
7 Inked it anew – it's a police representation (9)
8 Someone's plans are ruined by her cooking (5)
13 Supporter on burning issue has original thought (5-5)
15 Where to make a branch inspection? (9)
17 Stones are that messy, in ruins (9)
18 Roles revised after one member makes an earnest plea (8)
21 A girl wrong about nothing (her and her halo!) (6)
22 Explosive satirical composition (5)
24 In the saddle, aim to stand erect (5)
25 A number beheaded in uniform (4)

50

Across

1 Troops bustle, perhaps, to sort these out (7-5)
8 Man over the hill isn't totally bankrupt, we hear (3-4)
9 In Rome, I go on tour – it boosts one's image (3-4)
11 Bird I spotted with a locust (7)
12 Less respectable, having been given more umbrage? (7)
13 Irish saint turns to this girl (5)
14 Conductor in comeback repeated after opera (9)
16 Cost of transporting sodium from Port of Spain (9)
19 Party held by one animal for another (2-3)
21 Last longer in striking clothes (7)
23 Inspect main disaster in river (7)
24 Richard's enemy takes young Boer in (7)
25 Fetch from Montreal, I see (7)
26 Factors minimized in these original issues (5, 7)

Down

1 Research area used by Procrustes? (4, 3)
2 A canoe I manoeuvred in group of islands (7)
3 Bold soldier fighting, below peak (3, 6)
4 They're used to fence top Indian homes (5)
5 A part or arrangement in proportion (3, 4)
6 Ends part of school year in one (7)
7 Many racing over bridge in part of London (7, 5)
10 Spooner's noticing saint fed by naughty motorist (7-5)
15 Caught with drink, one's beaten by player (5, 4)
17 Perhaps a playful baby snake (7)
18 A mouthpiece conceals purpose in item for discussion (7)
19 Calm sort of current in river (7)
20 Ate among these? Change of diet is without point (7)
22 Arrest for quarrel (3-2)

51

Across

1 To do some haymaking this is carried (5)
4 Preserve by drying, thus, cat thrown in river (9)
9 Trees with sound quality provide building material (9)
10 Hot in the French resort for the recess (5)
11 Grounds of a Scottish mansion providing cover (6)
12 Careful to give breeding establishment financial
   acknowledgements (8)
14 Gallows – right tube entry maybe Marble Arch (6, 4)
16 Call round (4)
19 Outcry from a Shetland isle (4)
20 Style of reporting June sale, or it could be (10)
22 Lady Hester's carriage (8)
23 Mad crazy fool to provide the commercial target (6)
26 Smooth running of railways due to this cook? (5)
27 Not a hard condition of course, by no means strict (4-5)
28 Condition of seaworthy ship – or of its drunken crew?
   (9)
29 Number Nine's incomplete return of material (5)

Down

1 Paranormal communication the French way, yet without
  getting upset (9)
2 Dravidian tongue of many in the end (5)
3 Refuse to share this transport with Alfred Doolittle (4-4)
4 What might be indicative, contrariwise, of this fate (4)
5 Darling little dog that barked at King Lear (10)
6 Is a US lawyer able to unite this country? (6)
7 Recluse unravelled cipher in Thrace (9)
8 World Cup sides excluding the Spanish quoted in the
  betting (5)
13 The pervading mood all round the world (10)
15 No big ball arranged in the antipodean backwater (9)
17 Weapon for dealing with The Squeaker? (6-3)
18 Early woolly to go with balaclava helmet? (8)
21 Dwelling in which a letter is received (6)
22 Clog which, given time, could clog the works (5)
24 So order pretty maids in the nursery garden (5)
25 Goddess leads a double life? (4)

51

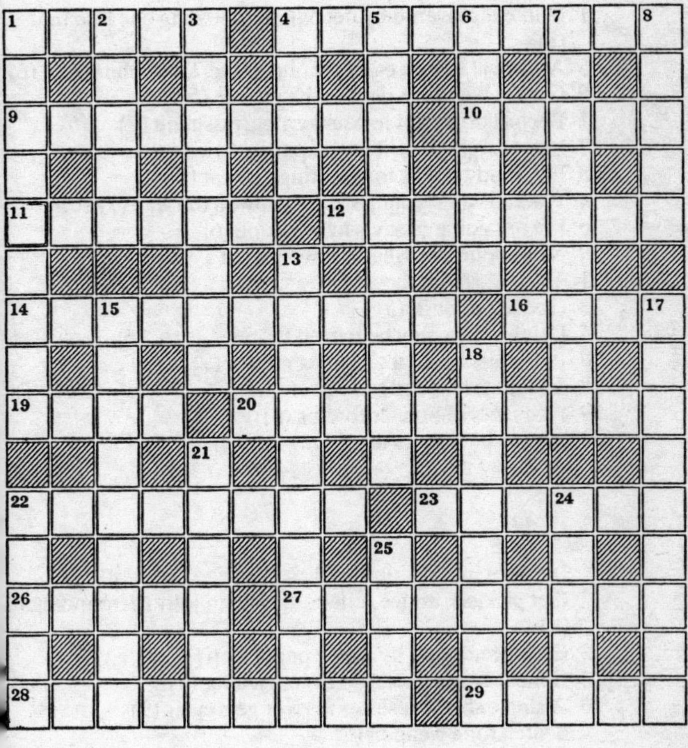

52

Across

1 Crime discovered by detectives following one into house (8)
5 Approval as expressed by one of the Trinity boatmen (6)
10 Carrier with flier right in the middle (5)
11 Record order apt to cause embarrassment (9)
12 Lightweight in split gave up title (9)
13 First Lady books for sporting contest (5)
14 Walked when young shaver showed the way (7)
16 I'm not going to say why it is sung (6)
19 Neighbour involves little woman in a row (6)
21 Squashes a relative (7)
23 One left in dark (5)
25 Drink which may be barred (9)
27 It provides in-flight reading matter (9)
28 Lad that is moved to perfection (5)
29 Fears loss of opener to slips (6)
30 Money held in trust not long ago (8)

Down

1 It comes in term-time and gives rise to mirth (8)
2 Get pickled, notice, after our time in jolly surroundings (9)
3 Creature caught by decoy put in trap (5)
4 Concluded notes about Italian leader (7)
6 A single ship's deserter in river gets clear (9)
7 Search for a weapon (5)
8 'When I am grown to man's—' (R. L. Stevenson) (6)
9 Comments by players – of the first elevens? (6)
15 Circus performer in Rome – Latin version (4, 5)
17 Covenant to supply cricketers without a square (9)
18 It may be felt in a liner (8)
20 Delicacy in NE City redevelopment (6)
21 Chastise the cat, possibly (7)
22 Minister provides remedy without a word of thanks in return (6)
24 Fifty soldiers turned up with the King afterwards (5)
26 This girl sounds a droop (5)

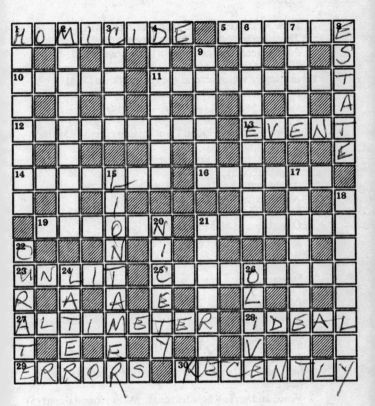

53

Across

1 Ex-works bikes for one-eyed bolt-makers (8)
5 This is no impediment for an air line (6)
10 A one-piece, reversible from knee to ankle (5)
11 No peace for the French captured by Custer's order (9)
12 Contest in which no one goes the distance (5, 4)
13 Intelligence shown by an assembly (5)
14 He dispenses the *Church Times* free (7)
16 Gives instruction in shorts (6)
19 He is said to have killed Duncan, and certainly Maria (using rope?) (6)
21 Like Cortez when not so high (3-4)
23 Organ-stop (5)
25 A rum mating call by a bird (4-5)
27 A spirited athlete, this gentleman (3-6)
28 Socially acceptable cooking herb in practice (5)
29 Once the sign of the freeholders (6)
30 Is the man dead, perhaps? More than likely! (8)

Down

1 Downpour making it difficult to see (8)
2 A Spanish gentleman – one right out of the Barcarolle, perhaps (9)
3 Seal held by Notary Public (5)
4 Remove surplus weight (7)
6 Sulphur smell round the gardens makes one cock-eyed (4-5)
7 Voice and verse – how fortunate Milton found them! (5)
8 Grudge gift when 30 (6)
9 Imposing Croat about on horseback (6)
15 A binding contract in bridge (9)
17 You can stay for nothing this height above sea-level (9)
18 Young gangster can hardly keep his hair on (8)
20 The king is due, coming by boat? (6)
21 English teak, or other hard wood (3-4)
22 Disgraceful complaint (6)
24 You'd have to sink pretty low to get through this dance (5)
26 The course of true love not running smooth (5)

This puzzle was solved within 30 minutes by 23 per cent of the competitors at the 1987 Glasgow regional final of the Times Collins Dictionaries Crossword Championship.

54

Across

1 Up at farm, big man beheaded birds (9)
6 Laugh at wolf (5)
9 The Song of Solomon as featured in conservatories? (7)
10 Minimal change to second dish (7)
11 Courts in European country, not US (5)
12 Follow girl into the plant (3-6)
14 Manipulate thickness (3)
15 Cards on the table for vote? (4, 2, 5)
17 Weapon for serious engraver (5-6)
19 Digit from West, presumably (3)
20 This paper's subordinate is in the right (9)
22 Nothing in foreign money held by French banks (5)
24 Have shortened golf club in porch (7)
26 Fired for editing badly (7)
27 Horse starting, perhaps, to throw monarch (5)
28 Endure return of blemishes? Too much for patient (4, 5)

Down

1 Former article of food (5)
2 Largely misplaced sensitivity (7)
3 People in serious offence (6, 3)
4 Insect caught in more imposing sort of clock (11)
5 Drink spirits for severe cold (3)
6 Did I crawl, perhaps, to religious teacher? (5)
7 Bunting helps aviator to land (7)
8 Preview given to feaster, possibly (9)
13 Transport sought by breeders (5, 6)
14 Photographs river I spotted in Cornish town (9)
16 Tough policies bringing bad luck! (4, 5)
18 Royal servant's direction to king in doubt (7)
19 Rook Oliver's taken with queen (7)
21 Fellow with gold a more blessed type (5)
23 Will finish with pained expression (5)
25 Tool with a point, to get special finish (3)

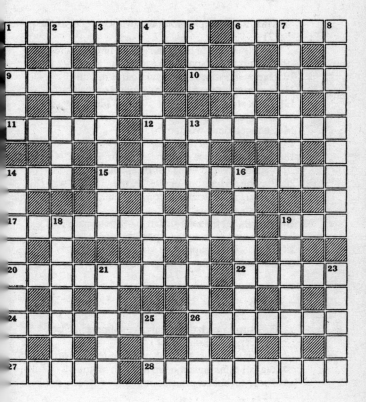

55

Across

1 Man, for example, accepted by theologian as the pattern (7)
5 Initially Carmen has divine voice but little craft (7)
9 Conspirator responsible for the highest rent? (5)
10 Happy in France to devour coarse biscuit (9)
11 Gunners trapped in boggy ground or marsh (6)
12 Blank state produced by 'Russian Flower' violin arrangement (8)
14 Changed daily woman (5)
15 Chap eating out needs some salt (9)
18 Wild pigeon race plummeted in America (5-4)
20 Vision is feeble – line has disappeared (5)
22 Playing an hautboy endlessly, the German way (8)
24 Raising agent to make pointed remark about Olympic finalists (6)
26 Instrument for long-distance off-peak calls (9)
27 Boxed jewel at end of a passage? (5)
28 Trousers, perhaps, not right in this silk (7)
29 Colourful display of buttons by worker (7)

Down

1 Creatures much put upon take slippers in case (4-5)
2 Like a party under cover? (7)
3 Left with repairs to Noah's vessel, found usurer (4, 5)
4 Way of thinking about an attempt on fourth of July (4)
5 These turbulent priests could have corns by tea-break! (10)
6 Teacher's pet practically (5)
7 Sculptor nominally welcome in Florence? (7)
8 Priest with a name for being a lover of lamb, we hear (
13 Regular tunnel not found in Winchester? (6-4)
16 Letting oneself down? It can be seen on the face (9)
17 Trojan hero's endless curse from outer part of cell (9)
19 A month to work as an ink-slinger (7)
21 Senior lady piano-scholar (7)
22 Stop at sea (5)
23 House wine receptacle to disappear (5)
25 Bite crisp biscuit (4)

56

Across

1 Lie about private American share recording (12)
9 Great painting? Far from it! (9)
10 Some of the most able men do better and better (5)
11 Have a preference for building on (4-2)
12 Stuff obtainable for ready money only (8)
13 Peasant citrus producer (6)
15 Write song that shows taste (8)
18 A controversial mathematician? (8)
19 Exceptional talent may be hidden (6)
21 Do they weigh only a little with punctilious people? (8)
23 Bird study by the river (6)
26 Remove bearings after a time (5)
27 Giving guidance, newspaper leader threw caution to the winds (9)
28 Tongue irritated by this medieval device (7, 5)

Down

1 Walker may well be up the pole! (7)
2 Article on for instance set-up in the city (5)
3 Beginning with fish, which is extraordinary (9)
4 Grub for a party (4)
5 The youngster, being green, ate out (8)
6 Black magic (5)
7 Purchase the pound, always over a period (8)
8 Approach a number before opening (6)
14 For those who want to get to the top by their own efforts (8)
16 Tea bar organized – can possibly provide transport (9)
17 Opinion held about people getting a flat (8)
18 Looked up to the woman doing security work (6)
20 Occupies several workers (7)
22 Statue representing sanctimonious Greek character (5)
24 Company about to declare capital (5)
25 Cat turning up on a sea-going vessel (4)

This puzzle was solved within 30 minutes by 50 per cent of the competitors at the 1987 Glasgow regional final of the Times Collins Dictionaries Crossword Championship.

57

Across

1 Ready to follow the flag for an allowance (3-5)
5 Privatise communications thus (6)
10 Early desert man (5)
11 Fashionable concern shown by a line to the hospital (9)
12 Three men to an office in Rome! (9)
13 A pine, from end to end (5)
14 Pretend to understand (4, 3)
16 No one scores off this girl (6)
19 Amuse oneself with bagatelle (6)
21 Cancel a run of The Ring (7)
23 The pirate king is finished (5)
25 Dots indicating gap in speech (9)
27 Non-flyer makes accountant thus careful (9)
28 Subject exemplified in story (5)
29 One who dies to support a cause (6)
30 Detective's featured in a dozen works (8)

Down

1 Separate prison sentence – not continuous (4-4)
2 One who finds fault can upset the selector (3-6)
3 Sulphuric acid eating away part of the linoleum (5)
4 He is in favour of the chosen people (7)
6 Relation arrives in the country (9)
7 Game in the shape of ducks in New Zealand (5)
8 Groyne hidden in sea holly (6)
9 A fine, sound state (6)
15 Volunteer to repay outsiders for church gifts (9)
17 Poor Belle's ill – Emily's twin (5, 4)
18 Staffs made from willows with chromium tops (8)
20 Make love to sweetheart disguised in Arden (6)
21 Examine breakdown (7)
22 Measure a drink after church outing (6)
24 Medieval way of saving face (5)
26 Memorial to engineer left one cold (5)

This puzzle was solved within 30 minutes by 18 per cent of the competitors at the 1987 Birmingham regional final of the Times Collins Dictionaries Crossword Championship.

58

Across

1 A sign is given by a musketeer (6)
5 Crazy thing for a careless scullion to do (8)
9 Old Aldershot establishment unsuitable for the David–Goliath fight (10)
10 Very large, it was a stepping-stone to heaven . . . (4)
11 . . . in such a legend here in Rome about a girl (8)
12 Much merriment when this saint consumes it (6)
13 Separate portion (4)
15 With volcanic rock nothing is in bad shape (8)
18 Many too old for reporter's work (8)
19 Topless wind or string instrument (4)
21 One and a half thousand fish? Nothing doing! (6)
23 A lad and girl gyrating in the old-time dance (8)
25 One once seen in and about Peru (4)
26 Winged jogger? (10)
27 This place has a crossing point for such cattle (8)
28 She made Hamlet mad (6)

Down

2 Writer makes loud appearance in part as Baron Corvo (5)
3 X marks the spot under this – it was the death of Balder (9)
4 The answer to its riddle was given by a man (6)
5 Foremost characters of clerical establishment (6, 2, 7)
6 Fountain nymph appears so in a square measure (8)
7 Minor eminence of King Oliver (5)
8 Domestic support for alumnus on the look-out (9)
14 Having upset the eggs I hop, getting out of the way (9)
16 Ophelia warned Laertes of its primrose path (9)
17 A grey and woolly jumper? Just so (8)
20 Boys' tipple (Johnson) would be port if it could (Bentley) (6)
22 Like Captain Flint blowing his top? (5)
24 Discharge of ambassador in strange circumstances (5)

59

Across

1 Jno. a forester (6, 4)
6 Over the side (4)
9 Madman full of wine in carriage (10)
10 A round in 5? It can be played (4)
12 Tax small business in a small way (4)
13 Try to get money from low land (5, 4)
15 A low-lying island, in the main (8)
16 Hot? No! Let's get moving (6)
18 He suffers from the withdrawal of two forms of transport (6)
20 Mournful-sounding architect? (8)
23 Sort of Western in which ponies can be seen (3, 6)
24 The horse to kick (4)
26 A good score is about one or two (4)
27 Florentine, perhaps – a climber ate it moving around (10)
28 Pattern or model – that covers it (4)
29 Vanessa a member of the Russian Navy? (3, 7)

Down

1 3's wife recorded finally in verse (4)
2 Of interest to those leading parties in Cumbria and Lancashire (7)
3 Organised London's entry as a writer (4, 8)
4 Those who wish to reach the other bank dry-shod must hurry (4, 2, 2)
5 Jack, for instance, gets on in time (6)
7 Involve brother in tree-climbing (7)
8 You could thus baffle Houdini – but not for long (3, 2, 5)
11 Wounded? This will buck you up (4, 2, 3, 3)
14 Bain-marie brings comfort to those retiring (7-3)
17 Army nurse got sick in army boats (8)
19 Worried rough becomes rougher (7)
21 Cake's name concealed, but not in code (2, 5)
22 Hear what goes into glass bottle (6)
25 Flatten a hill (4)

60

Across

1 Scratched old record? (10)
6 Small drink stain (4)
9 Second eleven from Germany – watch their inner pride (4-6)
10 River a fleet love to follow (4)
12 Formation of pelagic terns landing (7-5)
15 Weighing-machine could be set early to take old penny (9)
17 Blunder here yet panic does not begin (5)
18 Alternative easier part of Rossi aria . . . (5)
19 . . . rather like Bliss? (9)
20 Clarity of photograph (12)
24 Heroic record set by Olympic finalists (4)
25 Simenon's bureau, for example, with its back to the wall (10)
26 Lean nurse (4)
27 Early break – place for putting glue (10)

Down

1 Press promote and encourage enterprise (4)
2 White ill, out of order over a year (4)
3 This can give me Lisle's aria (12)
4 Spectacle for a great many (5)
5 Does he play to the gallery in the evening performance? (9)
7 This ground will not thaw – farmers opt out (10)
8 Toddler and runner of course (3-4-3)
11 Some grumbling about this condition? (12)
13 Selection for mixed sets (10)
14 Religious belief that followed Emma's coming out (10)
16 A 2p picker-up is one who would value it (9)
21 Mysterious how watercourse ends in lake (5)
22 Double note from Rudolph's girl (4)
23 Magistrate's bill (4)

Solutions

No. 1

ACROSS – 1, Reported; 5, Falter; 10, Scrub; 11, Overtones; 12, Dimension; 13, Carve; 14, Neutron; 16, Raisin; 19, Sticks; 21, Leghorn; 23, Altar; 25, Satirical; 27, Competent; 28, Gross; 29, Relate; 30, Assessor.

DOWN – 1, Resident; 2, Paramount; 3, Robin; 4, Emotion; 6, Attaching; 7, Tenor; 8, Russet; 9, Leaner; 15, Recurrent; 17, Iron Cross; 18, Analyser; 20, Sister; 21, Litotes; 22, Saucer; 24, Tamil; 26, Rogue.

No. 2

ACROSS – 1, Consommé; 5, Fledge; 9, Ante-post; 10, Impale; 12, Teems; 13, Dragonfly; 14, Object lesson; 18, Protectorate; 21, Desert rat; 23, Umber; 24, Memoir (Golda Meir); 25, Tomahawk; 26, Convey; 27, Defender.

DOWN – 1, Chaste; 2, Natter; 3, Opposable; 4, Misadventure; 6, Limbo; 7, Dwarfish; 8, Everyone; 11, Masterstroke; 15, Entourage; 16, Epidemic; 17, Houseman; 19, Aboard; 20, Broker; 22, Raise.

No. 3

ACROSS – 1, Bemuse; 4, Obeisant; 10, Certainly; 11, Human; 12, Decimal; 13, Partner; 14, Wield; 15, Tug of war; 18, Coachman; 20, Riser; 23, Fanatic; 25, Platoon; 26, Amber; 27, Baksheesh; 28, Essaying (gnome = aphorism); 29, Prayer.

DOWN – 1, Back down; 2, Miracle; 3, Spasmodic; 5, Buy a pig in a poke; 6, Ichor; 7, Ammonia; 8, Tundra ('ard nut (rev.)); 9, Uncle Tom's Cabin (alternative title, '*Life among the Lowly*'); 16, Forgather; 17, Trencher; 19, Omnibus; 21, Showery; 22, Efface; 24, Terry.

No. 4

ACROSS – 1, Gallon; 5, Kickshaw; 9, Confidante; 10, Goal; 11, Falsetto; 12, Upshot; 13, Away; 15, Turn tail; 18, Sideline; 19, Gate; 21, George (*Three Men in a Boat*, and automatic pilot); 23, Aircraft; 25, Rang; 26, Methodical; 27, Estrange; 28, Dry fly.

DOWN – 2, Aroma; 3, Life-style; 4, Nudity; 5, King of the Castle; 6, Chequers; 7, Sagas; 8, Anatomist; 14, Whitecaps; 16, Tiger-lily; 17, Linesman; 20, Arnold; 22, Roger; 24, Frail.

No. 5

ACROSS – 1, Beaufort scale; 9, Cathedral; 10, Crawl; 11, Ethic; 12, Burn; 13, Rows; 15, One-shot; 17, Origami; 18, Oil drum; 20, Negress; 21, Argo; 22, Anna; 23, Osier; 26, Titan; 27, Coastline; 28, Night-watchman.

DOWN – 1, Bachelor of Arts; 2, Aitch; 3, French horn; 4, Rarebit; 5, Salerno; 6, Arch; 7, Elaborate; 8, Plastic surgeon; 14, Diagnostic; 16, Enlighten; 19, Manx cat; 20, Niagara; 24, Ilium; 25, Snag.

No. 6

ACROSS – 1, Despot; 4, Blenheim; 10, Morceau; 11, Tripper; 12, Cryptogram; 13, Mete; 15, Andiron; 17, Gainsay; 19, Scrawls; 21, Cheques (CHE (It.) + QUE (Fr.) + S (Society)); 23, Hide; 24, Portuguese; 27, Bacilli; 28, Grandad; 29, Tolerant (Forbearing); 30, Shoddy.

DOWN – 1, Democrats; 2, Strayed; 3, Overthrown; 5, Lethargic; 6, Nail; 7, Empress; 8, Morse; 9, Bung; 14 Mimeograph; 16, Nestorian; 18, Yesterday (*Macbeth*, V. v. 22); 20, Radical; 22, Up-ended; 23, Habit; 25, Toga; 26, Slur.

No. 7

ACROSS – 1, Ambiance; 5, Dry bob; 10, Fair Maid of Perth (Katie Glover, Scott's heroine); 11, Isthmus; 12, Grapnel; 13, Cinnabar; 15, Terse; 18, Organ; 20, Celibate; 23, Encores; 25, Helicon; 26, Leonardo da Vinci; 27, Reefer; 28, Get ahead.

DOWN – 1, Affair; 2, Bristling (t (boat's stern) in brisling); 3, Almsman ((Ps)almsman); 4, Chips; 6, Replant; 7, Baron; 8, Beholder; 9, Doggerel; 14, Backside; 16, Reticence; 17, Modeller; 19, Narrate; 21, Bolivia; 22, Unbind; 24, Clove; 25, Hodge.

No. 8

ACROSS – 1, Substance; 6, Chime; 9, Abounds; 10, Planted; 11, Homer; 12, Irregular; 13, Tireless; 15, Help; 19, Inch; 20, Laughter; 23, Adventure; 24, Recur; 26, Airways; 27, Ireland; 28, Lodge; 29, Tangerine.

DOWN – 1, Spaghetti; 2, Bloom; 3, Tendrils; 4, Nastiest; 5, Expert; 6, Charge; 7, Intellect; 8, Eider; 14, Recovered; 16, Partridge; 17, Valerian; 18, Aggrieve; 21, Innate; 22, Outset; 23, Avail; 25, Coati.

No. 9

ACROSS – 1, Ithaca; 4, Scavenge; 10, Royal Navy; 11, Notch (initial letters); 12, Guipure; 13, Numeral; 14, Theta; 15, Ensemble; 18, Allegory; 20, Sedge; 23, Panache; 25, Scarlet; 26, Equip; 27, Roughshod; 28, Perverse; 29, Totnes.

DOWN – 1, Irrigate; 2, Haywire; 3, Calculate; 5, Cry one's eyes out; 6, Venom; 7, Natural; 8, Exhale (Exe round Kipling's Hal o' the Draft in *Puck of Pook's Hill*); 9, Pâté de foie gras; 16, Mustachio; 17, Testudos; 19, Languor; 21, Dolphin; 22, Upkeep; 24, Copse.

No. 10

ACROSS – 1, Flatter; 5, Augusta; 9, Reign; 10, Astronaut; 11, Weasel; 12, Agrestic; 14, Tolls; 15, Utterance; 18, Rhine wine; 20, Motet; 22, Especial; 24, Proper; 26, Therapist; 27, Nairn (i r(un) = single); 28, Postern; 29, Altered.

DOWN – 1, Fire-water; 2, Abigail; 3, Tennessee; 4, Road; 5, Altogether; 6, Gnome; 7, Spartan; 8, Attic; 13, Lusitanian; 16, Rembrandt; 17, Enthroned; 19, Impress; 21, Tipsier; 22, Estop; 23, Crave; 25, Stoa.

No. 11

ACROSS – 1, Grant; 4, Legislate; 9, Inheritor; 10, Neath; 11, Sunlit; 12, Foreland; 14, Nobel prize; 16, Stab; 19, Orts; 20, Unilateral; 22, Penelope; 23, Pimple; 26, Uncle; 27, Arabesque; 28, Billy-goat; 29, Theme.

DOWN – 1, Glissando; 2, Ashen; 3, Tortilla; 4, Lett; 5, Gorgonzola; 6, Sonnet; 7, Alabaster; 8, Ephod; 13, Grand piano; 15, Botanical; 17, Belvedere; 18, Strident; 21, Sleepy; 22, Plumb; 24, Pique; 25, Wait.

No. 12

ACROSS – 1, Powys (prisoners of war round Y(orkshire)); 4, Head start; 9, Acton Bell (Anne Brontë's pen-name); 10, Alpha; 11, Thrace; 12, Polonius ((Marco) Polo +in (rev.) US); 14, Somersault; 16 Stag (does = female deer); 19, Data; 20, Cloverleaf; 22, Barbados; 23, Enough; 26 Urals; 27, Axminster; 28, Bedfellow; 29, Whale.

DOWN – 1, Practised; 2, Water ('Here lies one whose name was writ in water', epitaph on Keats); 3, Sinecure; 4, Heep; 5, All for Love; 6, Shadow; 7, Appointee; 8, Thais; 13, Wall-to-wall; 15, Meter maid; 17, Gift-horse (Pegasus was given by Poseidon to Bellerophon); 18, Brand-new; 21, Maisie; 22, Blurb; 24, Ultra; 25, Smew.

No. 13

ACROSS – 1, Coleoptera; 6, Bath; 10, Pygmean; 11, Drummer; 12, Interlock; 13, Tithe; 14, Slope (Rev. Obadiah S., *Barchester Towers*); 15, Sunhelmet; 17, Freeboard; 20, Rotor; 21, Toxin; 23, Davenport; 25, Pianist; 26, Low-born; 27, Nash; 28, Prepayment.

DOWN – 1, Capri; 2, Lightsome; 3, One-armed bandit; 4, Tendons; 5, Redskin; 7, Admit; 8, Harvester ('Lend me your ears', *Julius Caesar*); 9, Rub the wrong way; 14, Safety-pin; 16, Metronome; 18, Auditor; 19, Develop; 22, X-rays; 24, Tenet.

No. 14

ACROSS – 1, Parade ground; 9, Ambulance; 10, Malta; 11, Allege; 12, Students; 13, Excite; 15, Graduate; 18, Relished; 19, Affect; 21, Commonly; 23, Camera; 26, Lithe; 27, Nutrition; 28, Manslaughter.

DOWN – 1, Placate; 2, Rebel; 3, Delegates; 4, Gang; 5, Overture; 6, Named; 7, Elongate; 8, Lassie; 14, Calamity; 16, Defeating; 17, Feelings; 18, Recall; 20, Trainer; 22, Opera; 24, Exist; 25, Etna.

No. 15

ACROSS – 1, Lorna (L(M)O(P)R(S)N(O)A(B)); 4, Edinburgh; 9, Checkmate; 10, Brian; 11, Hosea; 12, Planetary; 13, Residue; 15, Drawing; 18, Samoyed ('Every dog has its day'); 20, Juvenal; 21, Mont Blanc; 23, Cadge; 25, Pause; 26, Old stager; 27, Eye-shadow; 28, Dated.

DOWN – 1, Lock horns; 2, Reels; 3, Awkwardly; 4, Example; 5, Ireland; 6, Bible (George Borrow's *The Bible in Spain*); 7, Ruination; 8, Handy; 14, Simon Pure; 16, Advocated; 17, Goldenrod; 19, Diamond; 20 Jackdaw; 21, Maple; 22, Beech; 24, Digit.

No. 16

ACROSS – 1, Scrap; 4, Priestess; 9, Archangel; 10, Often; 11, Ross and Cromarty; 12, Agenda; 14, Barnyard; 17, Epistles; 19, Anonym (Corporal Nym, *Henry V*); 22, Saint Petersburg; 24, Avail; 25, Inspiring; 26, Steersman; 27, Genie.

DOWN – 1, Staircase; 2, Races; 3, Placard; 4, Pagoda; 5, Illyrian; 6, Showman; 7, Entertain; 8, Sandy; 13, Eliminate; 15, Demagogue; 16, Selenium; 18, Tattler; 20, Nesting; 21, Person; 22, Stays; 23, Union.

No. 17

ACROSS – 1, Scouse; 5, Proudhon; 9, Embracer; 10, Askari; 11, Piloting; 12, Pallid; 13, Emaciate; 15, Prod; 17, Bean ('He knows how many beans make five'); 19, Casemate; 20, Onsets; 21, Inkerman; 22, Louche; 23, Knuckles; 24, Stampede; 25, Tenuto.

DOWN – 2, Compiler; 3, Uprooted; 4, Enchilada; 5, Peregrine Pickle; 6, Upstage; 7, Headline; 8, Nail down; 14, Track suit; 15, Parolles; 16, Opuscula; 17, Bearskin; 18, Apparent; 19, Catchup.

No. 18

ACROSS – 1, Cupboard love (Old Mother Hubbard); 9, Rain-check; 10, Noble; 11, Cupola; 12, Swastika; 13, Lariat; 15, Brassard; 18, Prunella; 19, Boreas; 21, Overtime; 23, Beetle (in *Something of Myself* Kipling says he was the original of Beetle); 26, Titus; 27, Newmarket; 28, Record-player.

DOWN – 1, Caracal; 2, Primp; 3, Oscillate; 4, Reel; 5, Lukewarm; 6, Venus (*Our Mutual Friend*); 7, Abdicate; 8, Petard; 14, Roulette; 16, Stonewall; 17, Flamenco; 18, Pronto; 20, Sweater; 22, Taste (1 Samuel 14); 24, Tokay; 25, Owed.

No. 19

ACROSS – 1, Wednesday; 6, Cadet; 9, Equator (Puck's girdle round the earth); 10, Omnibus; 11, Extra; 12, Obedience; 13, Overcast; 15, Buss; 19, Eden; 20, Reappear; 23, Magnitude; 24, Learn; 26, Rhenish; 27, Rhubarb; 28, Hinge; 29, Mahlstick.

DOWN – 1, Woebegone; 2, Doubt; 3, Entrance; 4, Dormouse; 5, Yeomen; 6, Candid; 7, Debenture; 8, Taste; 14, Evergreen; 16, Springbok; 17, Research; 18, Applauds; 21, Divide; 22, Durham; 23, March; 25, Amati.

No. 20

ACROSS – 1, Smalls; 4, Asphodel; 10, Implore; 11, Garland; 12, Skateboard; 13, Ague; 15, Acetone; 17, Oersted; 19, Exegete; 21, Federal; 23, Clue; 24, Off-putting; 27, Embargo; 28, Umbrian; 29, Overrate; 30, Beagle.

DOWN – 1, Shipshape; 2, Appease; 3, Loose cover; 5, Sugar-loaf; 6, Hark; 7, Draught; 8, Ledge; 9, Veto; 14, Creditable; 16, Eyes front; 18, Diligence; 20, Equable; 22, Railing; 23, Credo; 25, Pout; 26, Brer.

No. 21

ACROSS – 1, Boracic; 5, Caracas; 9, Revenants; 10, Morse; 11, Maori; 12, Identical; 14, Figure of speech; 17, Intelligentsia; 21, Fortnight; 23, Riper; 24, Elian; 25, Town house; 26, Darkest; 27, Remodel.

DOWN – 1, Bireme; 2, Ravioli; 3, Continual; 4, Considering; 5, Cos; 6, Remit; 7, Coracle; 8, Stealthy; 13, Eiffel Tower; 15, Petersham; 16, Airfield; 18, Terrier; 19, Impound; 20, Orwell; 22, Nonce; 25, Tot.

No. 22

ACROSS – 1, Match play; 6, Palma; 9, Nearest; 10, Noisome; 11, Right; 12, Lie in wait; 13, Dripping; 15, Sick; 19, Yeti; 20, Jacobean; 23, The creeps; 24, Basis; 26, Aliquot; 27, Bribery; 28, Naked ((S)naked – unarmed); 29, Evergreen.

DOWN – 1, Man Friday; 2, Twang; 3, Heeltaps; 4, Let alone; 5, Yankee; 6, Pliant; 7, Look alive; 8, Adept; 14, In the pink; 16, King's Lynn; 17, Passable; 18, Cobbling; 21, Around; 22, Gentle; 23, Twain; 25, Suede.

No. 23

ACROSS – 1, Broadsword; 6, Omit; 9, Magistrate; 10, Trio (Beethoven's 'Archduke' Trio/riot); 12, Underclothes; 15, Collegian; 17, Sally; 18, Odour; 19, Sternness; 20, Practitioner; 24, Ibis; 25, Matchmaker; 26, Etna; 27, Metronomes.

DOWN – 1, Bump; 2, Orgy ((P)orgy); 3, Disintegrate; 4, Worse; 5, Reticence; 7, Marshalsea; 8, Trotskyist; 11, Cousin-german; 13, Accomplice (Alice Liddell); 14, Allocation; 16, Insatiate; 21, Occur; 22, Skim; 23, Eros.

No. 24

ACROSS – 1, Pitch; 4, Bedspread; 9, Petit four; 10, Datum; 11, Rosie (Laurie Lee, *Cider with Rosie*); 12, Money-bags; 13, Asunder; 15, English; 18, Kingdom; 20, Pioneer; 21, Gateposts; 23, Trail; 25, Apron; 26, Anatolian; 27, Saltpetre; 28, Negus.

DOWN – 1, Paperback; 2, Titus; 3, Hot-headed; 4, Bloomer; 5, Derange; 6, Paddy ('The Irish are a fair people', Dr Johnson); 7, Extradite; 8, Dumas; 14, Unnatural; 16, Ghost town (Arnold Ridley's play *The Ghost Train*); 17, Hard lines; 19, Miscast; 20, Passage; 21, Grass; 22, Pin-up; 24, Aping.

No. 25

ACROSS – 1, Portend; 5, Dracula; 9, Pacer; 10, Salvation; 11, Admiralty; 12, Tenor; 13, Knees; 15, Addressee; 18, Godliness; 19, Drift; 21, Icing; 23, Maharishi; 25, Detractor; 26, Crank; 27, Residue; 28, Cistern.

DOWN – 1, Pep-talk; 2, Recommend; 3, Error; 4, Displease; 5, Dolly; 6, Apartheid; 7, Union; 8, Aintree; 14, Shin-guard; 16, Dysphoric; 17, Ship-shape; 18, Guilder; 20, Thicken; 22, Ictus; 23, Metre; 24, Racks.

No. 26

ACROSS – 1, Fletcher; 5, Spider; 10, Evens; 11, Thespians; 12, Ditty-bags; 13, Queen; 14, Nursery; 16, Needle; 19, Elopes; 21, Rake-off; 23, Radii; 25, Indignant; 27, Horseback; 28, Axiom; 29, Desist; 30, Snookers.

DOWN – 1, Fielding; 2, Electoral; 3, Cushy; 4, Estuary; 6, Pipsqueak; 7, Drake; 8, Rising; 9, Nelson; 15, Emptiness; 17, Look-alike; 18, Oft-times; 20, Spiral; 21, Redskin; 22, Orchid; 24, Doris; 26, Guano.

No. 27

ACROSS – 1, Partner; 5, Arrears; 9, Relax; 10, Iroquoian (Seneca is one of the Iroquois peoples); 11, Oversight; 12, Hello; 13, Remit; 15, Unheard-of; 18, Puppeteer; 19, Tacks; 21, Typed; 23, Provender; 25, Hagridden; 26, Lunge; 27, Royalty; 28, Retreat.

DOWN – 1, Parlour; 2, Relief map; 3, Naxos (*Ariadne auf Naxos*); 4, Rain-gauge; 5, Afoot; 6, Roughcast; 7, Ariel; 8, Send off; 14, Treadmill; 16, Harpooner (Queequeg, in *Moby Dick*); 17, Decadence; 18, Pitcher; 20, Surfeit; 22, Piggy; 23, Paddy; 24, Eilat.

No. 28

ACROSS – 1, Extravagance; 8, Exploit; 9, Antares; 11, Elector; 12, Noisome; 13, Visor; 14, Ambulance; 16, Treachery; 19, Torch; 21, Overlay; 23, Went off; 24, Scamper; 25, Theatre; 26, Remonstrator.

DOWN – 1, Express; 2, Trotter; 3, Alternate; 4, Again; 5, Ant-hill; 6, Cartoon; 7, Reservations; 10, Scene-shifter; 15, Bayswater; 17, Elevate; 18, Calypso; 19, Tangent; 20, Rooster; 22, Yarns.

No. 29

ACROSS – 1, Olympus; 5, Octaves; 9, Scrapbook; 10, Ultra (marine); 11, Frail; 12, Tichborne; 14, Reconnaissance; 17, Easter offering; 21, Analgesia; 23, Table; 24, Twain; 25, Dog-collar; 26, Regnant; 27, Rudders.

DOWN – 1, Ossify; 2, Yardage; 3, Papillote; 4, Spontaneous; 5, Oak (OK round A); 6, Thumb; 7, Veteran; 8, Sea-fever; 13, Cliff-hanger; 15, Stratford; 16, Decanter; 18, Siamang; 19, Nebulae; 20, Hearts; 22, Gunga; 25, Dot.

No. 30

ACROSS – 1, Pitch-and-toss; 9, Astronaut; 10, Irene; 11, Armpit; 12, Camshaft; 13, Hookah; 15, Monastic; 18, Bull's-eye; 19, Abbess; 21, Artesian; 23, Stucco; 26, Loose; 27, Ill-gotten; 28, Desert island.

DOWN – 1, Pharaoh; 2, Totem; 3, Hooligans; 4, Noah (Hookah with no A H); 5, Tetrapod; 6, Swiss; 7, Repartee; 8, Celtic; 14, Oblation; 16, Albatross; 17, Sybarite; 18, Beagle; 20, Scorned; 22, Suede; 24, Cotta; 25, Plot.

No. 31

ACROSS – 1, Potlatch; 5, Seldom; 10, Corgi; 11, New Jersey; 12, Waste Land; 13, Drove; 14, Chamber; 16, Notify; 19, Cliché; 21, Marlene; 23, Bowls; 25, Miscreant; 27, Character; 28, Vital ((E)vita+l); 29, Sadder; 30, Flattery.

DOWN – 1, Pickwick; 2, Turns tail; 3, Alive; 4, Centaur; 6, Emendator; 7, Disco; 8, Mayhem; 9, Sweden; 15, Backstage; 17, Fremantle; 18, Mentally; 20, Enmity; 21, Mistral; 22, Abacus; 24, Weald; 26, Rivet.

No. 32

ACROSS – 1, Bed of roses; 6, Aged; 10, Brownie; 11, Repress; 12, Liege lord (lord = my!); 13, Range; 14, Embus; 15, Sometimes; 17, Witnessed; 20, Offal; 21, Equip; 23, Assessing; 25, Tutored; 26, Bloomer; 27, Even; 28, Blancmange (Blanc + man ((ho)g)e).

DOWN – 1, Babel; 2, Do one's bit; 3, Finders keepers; 4, Onerous; 5, Earldom; 7, Green; 8, Dispersal; 9, Operations room; 14, Enwreathe; 16, Muffin-man; 18, Scandal; 19, Dustbin; 22, Untie; 24, Gorge.

No. 33

ACROSS – 1, Backside; 5, Persia; 10, On the danger list; 11, Sackbut; 12, Options; 13, Mistrust; 15, Comma; 18, Ormer (Sea-ear); 20, Duchesse; 23, Embower; 25, Cheerio; 26, Tennis-court oath (Versailles, June 1789; see Brewer); 27, Yeomen; 28, Operatic.

DOWN – 1, Browse; 2, Catechism; 3, Sherbet; 4, Draft; 6, Erratic; 7, Sligo; 8, Artesian; 9, Agnostic; 14, Underact; 16, Miscreant; 17, Forestay; 19, Rawhide; 21, Elector; 22, Gothic; 24, Bingo; 25, Chump.

No. 34

ACROSS – 1, Hairpin; 5, Banking (Ban/king); 9, Nonet; 10, Altimeter; 11, Yarrow; 12, Forswore; 14, Oldie; 15, Leitmotiv; 18, Brasserie; 20, Dated; 22, Woodland; 24, Slalom; 26, Aborigine; 27, Ionic; 28, Hellene; 29, Kingdom.

DOWN – 1, Honeycomb; 2, Ignored; 3, Patroness; 4, Noah; 5, Bath Oliver; 6, Names; 7, Introit; 8, Gorse; 13, Florentine; 16, Medallion; 17, Vademecum; 19, Axolotl; 21, Taloned; 22, Wrath; 23, Loire; 25, Beak.

No. 35

ACROSS – 1, Castor; 4, Hangover; 10, Molière; 11, Aurochs; 12, Ambassador; 13, Turn; 15, Iterate; 17, Inhaler; 19, Engross; 21, Tessera; 23, Cash; 24, Sweetbread; 27, Marconi; 28, Praline; 29, Seconder; 30, Adders.

DOWN – 1, Campanile; 2, Soluble; 3, Overshadow (Eclipse, English racehorse that was never beaten); 5, Anatomist (James Bridie play); 6, Giro; 7, Victual; 8, Resin; 9, Leda; 14, Chessboard; 16, Erstwhile; 18, Readdress; 20, Gastric; 22, Eremite; 23, Comus; 25, Espy; 26, Loon.

No. 36

ACROSS – 1, Dog Latin; 5, Caucus (Cauc(as)us); 10, Crossword puzzle; 11, Eyelets; 12, Addenda; 13, Steerage; 15, Radii; 18, Lapse; 20, Optative; 23, Pikelet; 25, Complin; 26, Physiotherapist; 27, Rakish; 28, Almighty.

DOWN – 1, Dicker; 2, Goose step; 3, Austere; 4, Irons (gyves); 6, Asunder; 7, Cozen; 8, Scenario; 9, Adjacent; 14, Apostate; 16, Devil-fish; 17, Fly-paper; 19, Eclairs; 21, Timpani; 22, Snotty; 24, Kayak; 25, Creel.

No. 37

ACROSS – 1, Disarm; 5, Clematis; 9, Distance; 10, Sleepy; 11, Ear-muffs; 12, Cavell; 13, Assorted; 15, Fell; 17, Sobs; 19, Hoosegow; 20, Revamp; 21, Serenity (seren(dip)ity); 22, Sentry; 23, Academic; 24, Easement; 25, Dodgem.

DOWN – 2, Imitable; 3, Autumnal; 4, Manifesto; 5, Crease-resistant; 6, Mallard; 7, Trecento; 8, Spyglass; 14, Engarland; 15, Fair Isle; 16, Leavings; 17, Swanherd; 18, Bestride; 19, Humdrum.

No. 38

ACROSS – 1, Watch-dog; 9, Airliner; 10, Worn; 11, Thoroughfare; 13, Cinema; 14, Tetrapod; 15, Seaport; 16, Rockery; 20, Undersea; 22, Seneca; 23, Middle course; 25, Noah; 26, Two-piece; 27, Redheads ('The Red-headed League', Conan Doyle).

DOWN – 2, Amortise; 3, Centre spread; 4, Debonair; 5, Gavotte; 6, Fright; 7, Anna; 8, Friendly; 12, Frankincense; 15, Soul mate; 17, Observed; 18, Racecard; 19, Hanover; 21, Sweden; 24, Drop.

No. 39

ACROSS – 1, Palma; 4, Glassware; 9, New Forest; 10, Refer; 11, Aerate; 12, Inspirit; 14, Phenomenal; 16, Hang; 19, Edam; 20, Muscovites; 22, Dribbler; 23, Writhe; 26, Arena; 27, Assailant; 28, Tasteless; 29, Niger.

DOWN – 1, Pineapple; 2, Lower; 3, Adoption; 4, Glee; 5, Attendance; 6, Scraps; 7, Affirmant; 8, Egret; 13, Recuperate; 15, Examiners; 17, Gas-heater; 18, Aversion; 21, Oblate; 22, Draft; 24, Twang; 25, Isis.

No. 40

ACROSS – 1, Rehabilitate; 9, Jelly baby (Mrs Jellyby, *Bleak House*); 10, Romeo; 11, Intern; 12, Isabella (= greyish-yellow); 13, Entrée; 15, Geometry; 18, Borodino; 19, Advent; 21, Diogenes; 23, Alaska; 26, Issue; 27, Darwinian; 28, Stage-managed.

DOWN – 1, Rejoice; 2, Holst; 3, Boyfriend; 4, Leah; 5, Thyestes; 6, Throb; 7, Omelette; 8, Botany; 14, Tortoise; 16, Medallion; 17, Underdog; 18, Bodkin (*Hamlet*); 20, Trained; 22, Elect; 24, Swing; 25, Arum.

No. 41

ACROSS – 1, Garden suburb; 9, Observing; 10, Gnome; 11, Peruse; 12, Libelled; 13, Detail; 15, Measured; 18, Nepenthe; 19, Eroded; 21, Crockery; 23, Sweats; 26, Secco; 27, Stomacher; 28, Perambulator.

DOWN – 1, Grouped; 2, Riser; 3, Egression; 4, Said; 5, Beguiled; 6, Rogue; 7, Collared; 8, Tended; 14, Top-notch; 16, Screwball; 17, Charisma; 18, Nicest; 20, Desirer; 22, Krone; 24, Ashet; 25, Moab.

No. 42

ACROSS – 1, Divest; 4, Odometer; 10, Parsonage (the Brontës); 11, Norma, 12, Seltzer; 13, Storage; 14, Try on; 15, Gleaning; 18, Canoodle; 20, Ossia; 23, Volcano; 25, Railing; 26, Cheap; 27, Heathenry; 28, Tutelary; 29, Scarce.

DOWN – 1, Deposits; 2, Virelay; 3, Sforzando (writing S for Z and O in ZOO = SO); 5, Dress rehearsal; 6, Mango; 7, Terrain; 8, Reader; 9, Fairy godmother; 16, Neolithic; 17, Gargoyle; 19, Ailment; 21, Spinner; 22, Avocet; 24, Appal.

No. 43

ACROSS – 1, Cloche; 4, Implicit; 10, Uptight; 11, Shallop; 12, Coat-hanger; 13, Gimp; 15, Matinée; 17, Foolish; 19, Nest egg; 21, Lanyard; 23, Void (having no hearts); 24, Monday Club; 27, Withers; 28, Thoreau; 29, Landlady; 30, United.

DOWN – 1, Churchmen; 2, Outlast; 3, High-handed; 5, Masterful; 6, Loaf; 7, Cellini; 8, Top up; 9, Eton; 14, County Down; 16, Engrossed; 18, Hide-bound; 20, Stilton; 22, Ailment; 23, Vowel; 25, Date; 26, Peel.

No. 44

ACROSS – 1, Fatigue-party; 9, Imperfect; 10, Arena; 11, Blenny; 12, Open door; 13, Eyelid; 15, Isthmian; 18, Pathetic; 19, Arrack; 21, Pericope; 23, Blithe; 26, Cater; 27, Isinglass; 28, Writer's cramp.

DOWN – 1, Friable; 2, Topee; 3, Gerundive; 4, Exes; 5, Ante-post; 6, Train; 7, Veronica; 8, Patron; 14, Entirety; 16, Horologic (anag. CH GIRL OOO); 17, Misprint; 18, Papacy; 20, Knees-up; 22, Curer; 24, Tiara; 25, Bier.

No. 45

ACROSS – 1, Limbo; 4, Ascertain; 9, Shortstop; 10, Dhobi; 11, Clive; 12, Epitomise; 13, Useless; 15, Etching; 18, Thermos; 20, Lambent; 21, Back slang (Cosmo Gordon Lang); 23, Bogus; 25, Fishy; 26, Artichoke; 27, Gasholder; 28, Sweep.

DOWN – 1, Lose count; 2, Maori (7*dn* & I R O A M rev.); 3, On the beam; 4, Actress; 5, Capsize; 6, Rodeo; 7, Aborigine; 8, Naive; 14, Exercises; 16, Come-backs; 17, Go to sleep; 19, Seaward; 20, Lighter; 21, Befog; 22, Say-so; 24, Goose.

No. 46

ACROSS – 1, Marriage lines; 9, Sycophant; 10, Scene; 11, Caper; 12, Card (Arnold Bennett's *The Card*); 13, Itch; 15, Lombard; 17, Laertes; 18, Linocut; 20, Scherzo; 21, Shed; 22, Talc; 23, Selah; 26, Exile; 27, Stoolball; 28, Metamorphoses (Ovid).

DOWN – 1, Musical glasses; 2, Recap; 3, Importance; 4, Glanced; 5, Literal; 6, Nose; 7, Spectator; 8, Mephistopheles; 14, Methuselah; 16, Mannerism; 19, Transom; 20, Succour; 24, Leads; 25, Feat.

No. 47

ACROSS – 1, Whippoorwill; 8, Hackney; 9, Two-step; 11, Moisten; 12, Compose; 13, Izard; 14, Opponents; 16, Numerator; 19, Sober; 21, Handful; 23, Gallons; 24, Patella; 25, Assegai; 26, Heart to heart.

DOWN – 1, Wichita; 2, Ignited; 3, Paying out; 4, Optic; 5, Woodman; 6, Let-down; 7, Championship; 10, Pressure suit; 15, Paragraph (Para, or Belem, South American capital); 17, Manette (*A Tale of Two Cities*); 18, Ruffler; 19, Silesia; 20, Brought; 22, Least.

No. 48

ACROSS – 1, Malady; 4, Addition; 10, Dynasty; 11, Nictate; 12, Charioteer; 13, Fine; 15, Needled; 17, Salient; 19, Scourer; 21, Twister; 23, Peel; 24, Minute-hand; 27, Slaving; 28, Example; 29, Anterior; 30, Severs.

DOWN – 1, Medicines; 2, Lineate; 3, Distillery; 5, Dinner-set; 6, Inch; 7, Imagine; 8, Niece; 9, Eyot; 14, Illiterate; 16, Derring-do; 18, Tiredness; 20, Operant; 22, Trample; 23, Pasta; 25, Used; 26, Tier.

No. 49

ACROSS – 1, Sofia; 4, Foundling; 9, Boulevard; 10, Credo; 11, Egg-cup; 12, Brunette; 14, Chatterbox; 16, Skua; 19, Nibs; 20, Millimetre (*Thoroughly Modern Millie*, film); 22, Surplice; 23, Plough; 26, Utter; 27, Inverness; 28, Bombardon; 29, Sides.

DOWN – 1, Subdeacon; 2, Flung; 3, Adequate; 4, Flat; 5, Underworld; 6, Decent; 7, Identikit; 8, Goose (Cook someone's goose); 13, Brain-child; 15, Arboretum; 17, Amethysts; 18, Implores; 21, Gloria; 22, Squib; 24, Upend; 25, Even.

No. 50

ACROSS – 1, Trouble-spots; 8, Has-been (has bean); 9, Ego-trip; 11, Robinia; 12, Shadier; 13, Nadia; 14, Toscanini; 16, Cartagena; 19, Pi-dog; 21, Outwear; 23, Examine; 24, Saladin; 25, Realise; 26, Prime numbers.

DOWN – 1, Test bed; 2, Oceania; 3, Ben Battle (Thomas Hood); 4, Epées; 5, Pro rata; 6, Termini; 7, Charing Cross; 10, Parking-meter (Marking Peter); 15, Snare drum; 17, Rattler; 18, Agendum; 19, Placate; 20, Deities; 22, Run-in.

No. 51

ACROSS – 1, Toted; 4, Desiccate; 9, Limestone; 10, Niche; 11, Policy; 12, Studious; 14, Tyburn Tree (where Marble Arch now stands); 16, Ring; 19, Yell; 20, Journalese; 22, Stanhope; 23, Admass; 26, Broil; 27, Easy-going; 28, Tightness; 29, Ninon.

DOWN – 1, Telepathy; 2, Tamil; 3, Dust-cart (Shaw's *Pygmalion*); 4, Doom; 5, Sweetheart (*King Lear*, III. vi. 65); 6, Canada; 7, Anchorite; 8, Evens; 13, Atmosphere; 15, Billabong; 17, Grease-gun; 18, Cardigan; 21, Chalet; 22, Sabot; 24, Align; 25, Isis.

No. 52

ACROSS – 1, Homicide; 5, George (*Three Men in a Boat*); 10, Lorry; 11, Discomfit; 12, Renounced; 13, Event; 14, Toddled; 16, Shanty; 19, Adjoin; 21, Stepson; 23, Unlit; 25, Chocolate; 27, Altimeter; 28, Ideal; 29, Errors; 30, Recently.

DOWN – 1, Hilarity; 2, Marinaded; 3, Coypu; 4, Deduced; 6, Exonerate; 7, Rifle; 8, Estate; 9, Asides; 15, Lion tamer; 17, Testament; 18, Underlay; 20, Nicety; 21, Scourge; 22, Curate; 24, Later; 26, Olive (drupe).

No. 53

ACROSS – 1, Cyclopes; 5, Isobar; 10, Tibia; 11, Truceless; 12, Relay race; 13, Witan; 14, Chemist; 16, Briefs; 19, Corder (Macbeth, Thane of Cawdor, & William Corder, murderer of Maria Marten); 21, Off-peak; 23, Colon; 25, Wake-robin (arum); 27, Rum-runner; 28, Usage; 29, Yeomen; 30, Beheaded.

DOWN – 1, Cataract; 2, Caballero; 3, Otary; 4, Extract; 6, Skew-whiff; 7, Blest; 8, Resent; 9, Superb; 15, Indenture; 17, Freeboard; 18, Skinhead; 20, Rowing; 21, Oak-tree; 22, Scurvy; 24, Limbo; 26, Route.

No. 54

ACROSS – 1, Ptarmigan (Initial letters removed); 6, Scoff; 9, Solaria; 10, Platter; 11, Atria; 12, Dog-violet; 14, Ply; 15, Show of hands; 17, Stern-chaser; 19, Toe; 20, Thunderer; 22, Loire; 24, Veranda (VE/R and A); 26, Ignited; 27, Shyer; 28, Last straw.

DOWN – 1, Pasta; 2, Allergy; 3, Mortal sin; 4, Grandmother; 5, Nip; 6, Swami; 7, Ortolan; 8, Foretaste; 13, Goods trains; 14, Positives; 16, Hard lines; 18, Equerry; 19, Twister; 21, Donor; 23, Endow; 25, Awl.

No. 55

ACROSS – 1, Paisley (Pa/is/ley); 5, Coracle; 9, Casca (stabbed Caesar in the neck); 10, Garibaldi; 11, Morass; 12, Oblivion; 14, Lydia; 15, Manganite; 18, Stock dove; 20, Sight; 22, Autobahn; 24, Bicarb; 26, Alpenhorn; 27, India (E. M. Forster's *A Passage to India*); 28, Tussore; 29, Pageant.

DOWN – 1, Pack-mules; 2, Insured; 3, Loan-shark; 4, Yoga; 5, Corybantes; 6, Rabbi; 7, Cellini (Benvenuto Cellini); 8, Elian; 13, Smooth-bore; 16, Abseiling; 17, Ectoblast; 19, Octopus; 21, Grandma; 22, Avast; 23, Bingo; 25, Snap.

No. 56

ACROSS – 1, Registration; 9, Miniature; 10, Emend; 11, Lean-to; 12, Cashmere; 13, Rustic; 15, Penchant; 18, Wrangler; 19, Latent; 21, Scruples; 23, Falcon; 26, Erase; 27, Education; 28, Maltese Cross.

DOWN – 1, Rambler; 2, Genoa; 3, Startling; 4, Rout; 5, Teenager; 6, Obeah; 7, Leverage; 8, Advent; 14, Stairway; 16, Charabanc; 17, Tenement; 18, Washer; 20, Tenants; 22, Pieta; 24, Cairo; 25, Puss.

No. 57

ACROSS – 1, Pin-money; 5, Encode; 10, Rathe; 11, Infirmary; 12, Triumviri; 13, Along; 14, Make out; 16, Maiden; 19, Trifle; 21, Annular; 23, Rover; 25, Diaeresis; 27, Cassowary; 28, Liege; 29, Martyr; 30, Hercules (Poirot).

DOWN – 1, Part-time; 2, Nit-picker; 3, Oleum; 4, Elitist; 6, Narration; 7, Otago; 8, Eryngo; 9, Affirm; 15, Offertory; 17, Ellis Bell (Emily Brontë's pen-name); 18, Crosiers; 20, Endear; 21, Analyse; 22, Drachm; 24, Visor; 26, Relic.

No. 58

ACROSS – 1, Aramis; 5, Crackpot; 9, Glasshouse; 10, Ossa; 11, Hellenic; 12, Hilary; 13, Part; 15, Obsidian; 18, Coverage; 19, Lute; 21, Idling; 23, Galliard; 25, Inca; 26, Roadrunner; 27, Hereford; 28, Thelma.

DOWN – 2, Rolfe (Corvo's pen-name); 3, Mistletoe (Balder, Scandinavian god slain by twig of mistletoe); 4, Sphinx ('Man' was the answer to the Theban Sphinx's riddle); 5, Church of England; 6, Arethusa; 7, Knoll (Noll, Oliver Cromwell's nickname); 8, Observant; 14, Avoidance; 16, Dalliance; 17, Kangaroo; 20, Claret; 22, Irate (*Treasure Island*); 24, Rheum.

No. 59

ACROSS – 1, Little John; 6, Left; 9, Deportment; 10, Oboe; 12, Scot; 13, Touch down; 15, Atlantis; 16, Stolen; 18, Martyr; 20, Plangent; 23, New Forest; 24, Hack; 26, Pair; 27, Italianate; 28, Norm; 29, Red Admiral.

DOWN – 1, Lady; 2, Topical (TO + initials); 3, Lord Tennyson; 4, Jump to it; 5, Honour; 7, Embroil; 8, Tie in knots; 11, Shot in the arm; 14, Warming-pan; 17, Flotilla; 19, Rowdier; 21, En clair; 22, Mettle; 25, Fell.

No. 60

ACROSS – 1, Palimpsest; 6, Spot; 9, Self-regard (elf = eleven in German); 10, Arno; 12, Resting-place; 15, Steelyard; 17, Error; 18, Ossia; 19, Paradisal; 20, Transparency; 24, Epic; 25, Escritoire; 26, Tend; 27, Greenstick (putting as in golf).

DOWN – 1, Push; 2, Lily; 3, Marseillaise; 4, Sight; 5, Serenader; 7, Permafrost; 8, Two-year-old; 11, Appendicitis; 13, Assortment; 14, Persuasion (Jane Austen's novel, published after *Emma*); 16, Appraiser; 21, Eerie; 22, Mimi (*La Bohème*); 23, Beak.